MOON

52 THINGS TO DO IN

LOS ANGELES

TEENA APELES

CONTENTS

Day Trips and Getaways

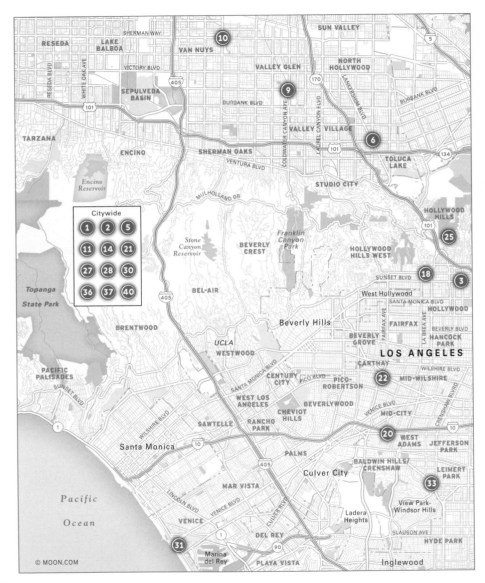

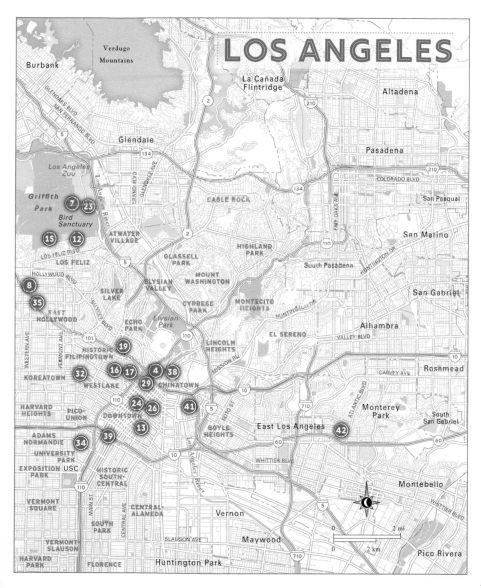

LOS ANGELES

PACIFIC

OCEAN

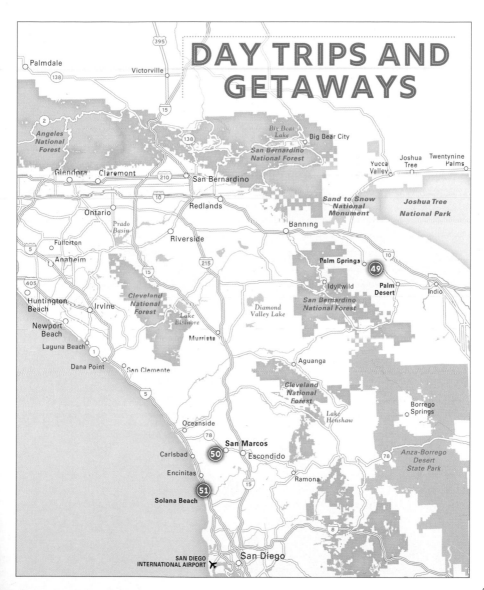

DAY TRIPS AND GETAWAYS

THIS IS MY L.A.

Los Angeles is a complex and magical city. Its varied landscape of coastline, mountains, wetlands, valleys, and waterways are wonders to explore. Yes, the endless urban sprawl and winding freeway mazes can be frustrating, but they can be thrilling, too. As you navigate L.A., you never know what the day may bring.

What really makes our city's heart beat like no other are the people who call it home, many of whom have dreams of something greater and refuse to be defined or categorized in one way. As the whole world knows, we embrace imagination and experimentation, but also preservation. You'll see these values come through in a multitude of ways, from our architecture to our nightlife. We prize our multiethnic population, which has succeeded in protecting beloved traditions as well as creating—out of the city's intermingling of influences—new cuisines, art, and popular phenomena that are quintessentially L.A. The sheer volume of cultural offerings may feel overwhelming, but locals like it that way.

I was born in L.A., a child of immigrants, at a hospital with a view of the Hollywood Sign. I am raising another proud Angeleno who helps me see the city anew each day. But you don't need to have Los Angeles on your birth certificate or follow every media-worthy trend to appreciate it. You just need a willingness to seek out the range of what makes this city so extraordinary—its gum-marked pavements and magnificent sunsets, street food fare and famous restaurants immortalized in song, concrete-lined river and sparkling ocean waters.

The following are 52 ways to experience Los Angeles throughout the year. Go forth by car, by public transit, by bike, and on foot. Each mode of transportation will reveal something new and unexpected.

Downtown L.A. skyline

TO DO LISTS

Iconic L.A.

3 Feast on **famous chicken in Hollywood**

7 Find **Griffith Park's** hidden gems

8 Sample late-night **tacos on Sunset Boulevard**

9 See California's overlooked history at the
Great Wall of Los Angeles

10 Revel in L.A. car culture at **Van Nuys Cruise Night**

11 Watch **movies in historic theaters**

14 Get your photo taken by a **local legend**

15 See stars at L.A. County's **observatories**

23 Bike along the **L.A. River**

24 Tour **Downtown architecture**

30 Find unexpected art and culture in **L.A.'s cemeteries**

Entertainment and Events

① Cycle down car-free streets during **CicLAvia**

② See **all-female mariachi bands**

④ Dance under the stars at **Chinatown Summer Nights**

⑤ Sharpen your **comedy** chops, practice **magic,** and join the **circus** . . . It's L.A.

⑥ Sing along at **Idle Hour's drag brunch**

⑩ Revel in L.A. car culture at **Van Nuys Cruise Night**

⑪ Watch **movies in historic theaters**

㉑ Celebrate life and death during **Día de los Muertos**

㉗ Check out the **L.A. jazz** scene

㉙ Learn some new moves at **Dance DTLA**

㉝ Dance while you browse at **Crenshaw Mall's Saturday markets**

㊾ Take an **art road trip in the Coachella Valley**

Food and Drink

Get Outside

1 **Cycle down car-free streets** during CicLAvia

7 Find **Griffith Park**'s hidden gems

17 Catch skyline views from **Vista Hermosa Natural Park**

19 Ride a **swan boat**

23 Bike along the **L.A. River**

25 Go on a lakeside **walk beneath the Hollywood Sign**

31 Stroll around the **Venice Canals**

43 Picnic and park-hop in **seaside San Pedro**

44 Wander the tide pools at **Abalone Cove Beach**

45 Play in the **snow and sand on the same day**

46 Pick fresh produce from **SoCal farms**

47 Enjoy **nearby nature and small-town charm in Ojai**

50 Captain your own boat on **Lake San Marcos**

52 Spend the night on **Catalina Island**

Art and Culture

2 See **all-female mariachi bands**

9 See California's overlooked history at the *Great Wall of Los Angeles*

11 Watch **movies in historic theaters**

12 Take a walking tour of **Los Feliz architecture**

14 **Get your photo taken** by a local legend

20 Shop for **art and wine in West Adams**

21 Celebrate life and death during **Día de los Muertos**

24 Tour **Downtown architecture**

27 Check out the **L.A. jazz scene**

30 Find unexpected art and culture in **L.A.'s cemeteries**

34 Delve into the world's largest LGBTQ collection at **ONE Archives**

36 Get creative with **local artisans**

42 Catch rising SoCal stars at the **Vincent Price Art Museum**

49 Take an **art road trip** in the Coachella Valley

Neighborhoods and City Streets

4 Dance under the stars at **Chinatown** Summer Nights

8 Sample late-night tacos on **Sunset Boulevard**

10 Revel in L.A. car culture at **Van Nuys** Cruise Night

12 Take a walking tour of **Los Feliz** architecture

13 Buy fresh blooms in the **Flower District**

16 Tour **Historic Filipinotown** by Jeepney

18 Go on a bar crawl at **Hollywood** hotels

20 Shop for art and wine in **West Adams**

22 Eat with your hands in **Little Ethiopia**

24 Tour **Downtown** architecture

26 Enjoy the cultural feast of the **Piñata District**

31 Stroll around the **Venice** Canals

35 Go international bakery-hopping in **East Hollywood**

41 Take a Metro tour of **Boyle Heights**

For All Ages

1 Cycle down car-free streets during **CicLAvia**

7 Find **Griffith Park's hidden gems**

15 See stars at L.A. County's **observatories**

19 Ride a **swan boat**

25 Go on a lakeside **walk beneath the Hollywood Sign**

26 Enjoy the cultural feast of the **Piñata District**

29 Learn some new moves at **Dance DTLA**

43 Picnic and park-hop in **seaside San Pedro**

44 Wander the **tide pools at Abalone Cove Beach**

45 Play in the **snow and sand on the same day**

46 Pick fresh produce from **SoCal farms**

51 Ride the *Pacific Surfliner* to Solana Beach

Get Out of Town

43 Picnic and park-hop in seaside **San Pedro**

44 Wander the tide pools at **Abalone Cove Beach**

45 Play in the **snow and sand on the same day**

46 Pick fresh produce from **SoCal farms**

47 Enjoy nearby nature and small-town charm in **Ojai**

48 Get away to **Santa Barbara**

49 Take an art road trip in the **Coachella Valley**

50 Captain your own boat on **Lake San Marcos**

51 Ride the *Pacific Surfliner* to **Solana Beach**

52 Spend the night on **Catalina Island**

1 Cycle down car-free streets during CicLAvia

Entertainment and Events • Get Outside • For All Ages

Why Go: Enjoy the rare opportunity to enjoy miles of car-free streets in the city.

Where: Citywide

Timing: CicLAvia takes place on Sundays a few times a year, typically 9am-4pm. The annual Heart of LA event generally takes place in October. Check the website for schedules and access points.

When it comes to exploring the city's streets and neighborhoods, no event is as thrilling as the no-cars affair **CicLAvia** (213/355-8500, www.ciclavia.org, free). Since 2010, the program, which temporarily closes roads to motor vehicle traffic, has attracted thousands of people to enjoy city streets by foot, bike, scooter, stroller, wheelchair, skateboard, and more. Prior to its launch, the only other way to experience open streets like this was by participating in the L.A. Marathon. But as organizers will remind you, CicLAvia is not a race, but a journey—where everyone wins.

While all are welcome to join so long as their method of transport is human-powered, bicyclists dominate the events. The first route that kicked off CicLAvia was the "Heart of LA." It was one of the most incredible days I've ever spent in Los Angeles. Part of the joy was just seeing bikers of all ages converging on the route from all directions, with riders excitedly screaming and hollering, including kids on tricycles pedaling with fury, like they owned the road. On CicLAvia days, we all do.

The **Heart of LA ride** has become an annual event. The exact route varies year to year, but it guides riders in and around Downtown and surrounding neighborhoods, often by cultural sites like City Hall, Little Tokyo's Japanese American National Museum, Chinatown's Central Plaza, and Boyle Heights' Mariachi Plaza. A recurring **South L.A. event** has led participants to the Watts Towers, Promenade of Prominence Walk of Fame, Ted Watkins Memorial Park, Dunbar Hotel, Central Avenue Jazz Park, and Bowers Retail Square.

riders at the TCL Chinese Theatre on the Hollywood Walk of Fame

bicyclists on Wilshire Boulevard

Other CicLAvia events vary. Past events have included Meet the Hollywoods (West to East Hollywood) and Iconic Wilshire Boulevard. Others have taken people through neighborhoods in Greater L.A. County like Wilmington, Culver City, and Pasadena.

On each route—which range around 3-7 miles—CicLAvia establishes hubs, often around Metro stations, public parks, or landmarks, where live entertainment also often takes place. Local bands, DJs, and dancers might be among the scheduled attractions, but welcome guerilla performances also occur simultaneously along the routes. There are water and bike tune-up stations, bathrooms, first-aid services, and photo booths. Keep an out for **Las Fotos Project** (http://lasfotosproject.org), an organization that works with teenage girls from communities of color to empower them and elevate their voices through the medium of photography; one of my best family photos was taken (for free!) by one of these talented photographers. You can also check out independently owned shops along each route.

For me, the climax of a CicLAvia ride occurs when you move from a narrow neighborhood street to a crowded hub or famous landmark amid an expanse of smiling participants. It

author with her family at the 2019 Heart of LA ride

always punctuates an "I love L.A." moment, making me wonder, "Why can't every day be like this?" The diversity of the city's residents, neighborhoods, and architecture is on full display. CicLAvia offers some of the best people-watching in town; don't be surprised to find yourself riding or walking alongside a person in an armadillo costume nearly the size of a small car, a 10-foot-high unicycle rider, or the mayor of Los Angeles. When I asked the CicLAvia team about their favorite sightings, they said, "A skateboarding granny [regular participant Swee (Ool) Woo], a pack of longboarders, a formal dinner table set for eight, groups on wheelchairs, roller derby teams, and stroller parties."

Some tips: Remember to wear comfortable shoes and attire, bring a water bottle to stay hydrated, and wear a hat to keep cool. If you're hiking, check your chain, tires, and brakes to ensure everything is in good shape. It's always smart to pack your own pump and tools, and to wear a helmet. If you don't have your own bike, there are usually **Metro bikes** (http://bikeshare.metro.net) at the hubs. CicLAvia also offers free pedicab rides at each hub for anyone who wants a ride to the next hub. The organization posts a set of rules to ensure the safety and enjoyment of all. It's fun to kick off your ride right when the route opens at 9am to be at the front of the pack, but it's also awesome to start later in the day and be in the midst of a sea of bikers.

See you at the next one!

2 See all-female mariachi bands

Entertainment and Events • Art and Culture

Why Go: L.A.'s numerous award-winning all-female mariachi bands are part of a revolutionary movement in music, and seeing them perform live is enthralling and inspiring.

Where: Citywide

Timing: These mariachi bands play at different city festivals throughout the year. You can also catch shows by following the bands' social media or hiring them for a party!

Mariachi music is an integral part of Los Angeles life. You'll hear Mexico's traditional folk music playing in passing cars. Live performances take place on public plazas and at local restaurants. And then there's my favorite way to experience mariachi music: serendipitously happening upon a band rehearsing in a public park or walking down a neighborhood street to serenade a birthday celebrant. But while every Angeleno has seen a mariachi band somewhere in the city, not everyone has seen an all-female mariachi band play—and they should.

L.A. is home to a vibrant mariachi scene in general, with such popular events as the **Mariachi USA festival** (http://mariachiusa.com, summer) held annually at the Hollywood Bowl and bands playing daily at Boyle Heights' **Mariachi Plaza.**

But it also proudly boasts a number of all-female bands. Remember these names: **Mariachi Reyna de Los Angeles** (http://reynadelosangelesmusic.com), **Mariachi Las Adelitas** (www.mariachilasadelitas.com), **Las Colibrí** (http://colibrient.com), **Mariachi Divas de Cindy Shea** (www.mariachidivas.com), **Mariachi Las Catrinas** (www.facebook.com/mariachilascatrinas), **Mariachi Lindas Mexicanas** (www.facebook.com/mariachilindasmexicanas), **Mariachi Nuevo Mujer 2000** (www.mariachinuevomujer2000.com), and **The Mariachi Conservatory All Female Ensemble** (http://themariachiconservatory.org). Almost all of these bands were founded by and are led by women, and they are each making history by playing music traditionally played by men—bringing their own unique

▲ Las Colibrí at the 57th Annual L.A. County Holiday Celebration at the Music Center

International Mariachi Women's Festival at the San Gabriel Mission Playhouse

The Mariachi Conservatory All Female Ensemble at a practice session

takes on the genre through their choices of instruments and costumes, giving contemporary songs the mariachi treatment, and writing their own music from a woman's point of view.

Witnessing female artists forging a new tradition evokes a profound sense of joy and empowerment. Imagine a chorus of upwards of 12 female voices singing mariachi songs in unison on stage, or an all-female trumpet section playing in a plaza or restaurant. They bring a completely different sound and energy to a live performance. Most bands don their colorful and ornately decorated *traje de charro* suits with pride, while some opt for more feminine attire, such as skirts and blouses. Other musical and artistic choices—from the number of band members to how the musicians do their makeup—distinguish the bands. Despite a long history of watching on the sidelines or being token members of male groups, these musicians have emerged as Grammy and Latin Grammy winners for their craft, which started with their live performances.

You might catch the bands at venues such as the **San Gabriel Mission Playhouse** (320 S. Mission Dr., San Gabriel, 626/308-2865, http://missionplayhouse.com), just east of the city, which hosts the annual **International Mariachi Women's Festival** (www.mariachiwomen.org, Mar.); **The Ford** (2580 Cahuenga Blvd. E., 323/850-2000, www.theford.com); **Music Center** (135 N. Grand Ave., 213/972-7211, www.musiccenter.org); and **La Plaza de Cultura y Artes** (501 N. Main St., 213/542-6200, http://lapca.org). With each appearance, they grow their fan base and inspire new generations of girls and women to take up mariachi instruments or start their own mariachi bands.

Check out the bands' respective websites or social media to see where they'll play next, view past performances, or book a band for your next special occasion!

3 Feast on famous chicken in Hollywood

Iconic L.A. • Food and Drink • For All Ages

Why Go: Sate your chicken cravings at these local institutions that are so good they've inspired songs.

Where: Hollywood • Metro bus 2 or LADOT Hollywood/Wilshire Southbound DASH to Sunset/Gower (Roscoe's) • Metro bus 2 to Sunset/Normandie (Zankou Chicken)

Timing: Roscoe's and Zankou are open morning until midnight. Get your order to go or eat in to soak up the scenes.

Being in the know about two casual chicken-centric eateries in the city will immediately identify you as a local (or an L.A. insider). Each has multiple locations in Southern California, but the oldest L.A. incarnations are the most iconic—both are frequently referenced in pop culture. They're located in Hollywood, just over a mile apart, touting secret recipes that have lasted the test of time and drawing people from near and far. If you're ambitious, you could try both in a day, brunching at Roscoe's, catching a movie in the area or walking off the hearty meal in nearby green spaces, then grabbing dinner at Zankou.

Soul-food chain **Roscoe's House of Chicken & Waffles** (1514 N. Gower St., 323/466-7452, www.roscoeschickenandwaffles.com) has been name-checked in songs by numerous hip-hop and rap artists, including Nicki Minaj and Tyler, The Creator. Stevie Wonder and Natalie Cole visited in the '70s. Snoop Dogg is a longtime regular. Tupac Shakur's 1996 music video for "To Live and Die in L.A." ends with a food fight in front of Roscoe's Hollywood location, and that joy you see on the crowd's faces? That's the spirit of the place. Originally from Harlem, Herb Hudson opened the first Roscoe's in Long Beach (since closed) in 1975 before opening this outpost, featuring interior wood paneling and neon signage, near the Hollywood Walk of Fame and movie studios. The Southern-style, deliciously crispy chicken and waffles found fans in no time. People also rave about the mixed greens, corn bread, yams, biscuits, and mac and cheese. A classic "Scoe's" order comes with two pieces of fried chick-

Zankou Chicken platter

rotating spits at Zankou Chicken

iconic Roscoe's sign

fried chicken and waffles at Roscoe's

en—you can choose which parts of the chicken you want—and two waffles. Add on one of Roscoe's signature layered juice drinks: the Sunrise (orange juice with lemonade) or Sunset (fruit punch with lemonade). Without fail, at any hour, this location will have a line of people waiting outside, with lots of couples and families and everyone else under the sun just smiling ear to ear and talking up a storm. It might take around 15-20 minutes for a table, but the people-watching here is great, and you can check out the action while you wait.

While it underwent a major renovation in recent years, you might recognize **Zankou Chicken** (5065 Sunset Blvd., 323/665-7845, www.zankouchicken.la) from Childish Gambino's (aka Donald Glover's) 2015 music video for "Sober," featuring him dancing on the eatery's tables. Native Angeleno Beck sang in memorable fashion about Zankou Chicken in the 1999 song "Debra." The Iskenderian family first opened Zankou Chicken in Beirut, Lebanon, in 1962. They eventually sold it, moved to Los Angeles, and, in 1984, opened this Sunset Boulevard location in an area that later became designated as Little Armenia, serving their beloved rotisserie chicken and secret garlic sauce. My parents have been ordering

exterior of Zankou Chicken on Sunset Boulevard

takeout from Zankou Chicken ever since, and passed their love for it on to their daughters and grandkids. As noted above its entrance, the restaurant is "Open 364 Days"; the only day it's closed is April 24, Armenian Genocide Remembrance Day. There are often lines here, but service is fast and there are usually open tables. Order from the stainless-steel counter that runs the length of the restaurant, where the rotating spits will tempt you from behind the cashier. Get the rotisserie chicken, in any form; it's juicy and flavorful, and you can take your pick of white or dark meat. My family prefers to get individual chicken plates, which include the garlic sauce as well as hummus, tomatoes, pickled turnips, yellow peppers, and pita bread. We always order extra garlic sauce, plus a side of tabbouleh and basmati rice. It can get messy, and that garlic sauce will linger on your breath and hands for a while—but it's worth it.

Connect with . . .

7 Find Griffith Park's hidden gems

11 Watch movies in historic theaters

25 Go on a lakeside walk beneath the Hollywood Sign

4 Dance under the stars at Chinatown Summer Nights

Entertainment and Events • Neighborhoods and City Streets • For All Ages

Why Go: This seasonal all-ages experience celebrates Chinese culture and is hands-down one of the best outdoor dance parties of the year—replete with confetti cannons.

Where: Chinatown, along N. Broadway Ave. and N. Hill St. between Bernard St. and W. College Ave. • Metro L Line (Gold) to Chinatown Station • Metro bus 81 to Hill/College

Timing: This event takes place 5pm-midnight one Saturday a month June-August. Finding parking gets more difficult (and more expensive) over the course of the night; consider carpooling, using a ride-hailing service, or taking public transit.

Live in L.A. long enough and you are likely to have a favorite Chinatown memory—I have many. As a child it was walking across Central Plaza with my Filipino Chinese *lola* (grandmother) to purchase steamed pork buns, or *siopao* (as Filipinos call them), at Wonder Bakery and walking farther down Broadway to pick up fresh strawberry cake at Phoenix Bakery for every birthday celebration. Since 2010, many Angelenos have one treasured memory in common: **Chinatown Summer Nights** (213/680-0243, http://chinatownsummernights.com, free), a multisensory, multiblock party held monthly in season. As the San Gabriel Valley became the destination for more varied and authentic Chinese food, the event was launched to attract new people to the area and bring back past visitors. The summer series has brought crowds to patronize the local businesses, but also something arguably more vital: Angelenos of all ages and backgrounds, partying in the neighborhood together and taking in all of its offerings.

While it has gotten more corporate over the years, the outdoor event remains a joy, whether you're with friends, on a date, or have kids or lively grandparents in tow. Chinatown's colorful neon signs and rows of hanging lanterns seem to shine brighter on these glorious Saturday evenings, when a neighborhood that usually feels like a dusty Hollywood

reveler collecting confetti in the Central Plaza

Chinatown Summer Nights

⌃ neon signage in the Central Plaza

⌃ Bruce Lee statue by artist Zhong Zhiyuan in Chinatown's Central Plaza

set is transformed into the bustling heart of Los Angeles, with thousands of people filling its plazas. There are music and dance performances celebrating Chinese culture, culinary demonstrations, arts and crafts activities, and vendors selling goods. You'll generally find a **food-truck parade** serving different cuisines on Jung Jing Road, where you can also snap a pic with the **Bruce Lee statue** (Jung Jing Rd. at Sun Mun Way). The **LA Weekly Live Music Stage** features local bands in the parking lot behind Wonder Bakery (943 N. Broadway). But we all know the place to be at 8pm: the dance floor in **Central Plaza** (943-951 N. Broadway), where happy Angelenos dance and revel while setting off confetti cannons in all directions as KCRW DJs spin. Join in the fun by purchasing your own confetti cannons—available in multiple sizes—from stores in the plaza! (Just watch your step to make sure you don't trip over a kid collecting confetti from the floor.)

It gets cool at night, so bring a jacket. When you need to get away from the hubbub, slip into a restaurant for a meal. Our family and friends stick to tried-and-true favorites: **Full House Seafood Restaurant** (963 N. Hill St., 213/617-8382, www.fullhouseseafood.com) for snow pea leaves, salt-and-pepper shrimp (request no shell), and the house special pan-fried noodles; **Golden Dragon Restaurant** (960 N. Broadway, 213/626-2039, www.goldendragonla.com) for dumplings and a mango pudding palate cleanser; and **Yang Chow** (819 N. Broadway, 213/625-7901, www.yangchow.com), where everyone loves the slippery shrimp.

You'll arrive home with remnants of the night: colorful strips of confetti in your clothes or bag. Hopefully you had such a good time that you're inclined to save them.

Connect with . . .

14 Get your photo taken by a local legend

37 Steep yourself in the city's teahouse culture (Steep LA)

40 Savor L.A.'s multicultural flavors at celebrated family-run eateries (The Little Jewel of New Orleans Grocery & Deli)

5 Sharpen your comedy chops, practice magic, and join the circus . . . It's L.A.

Entertainment and Events • Art and Culture

Why Go: Take classes in various art forms from veterans of the craft in the entertainment capital of the world.

Where: Citywide

Timing: Classes are offered at these institutions throughout the year and can range from an hour to six weeks.

If you've ever dreamt of taking to the stage as an aerialist, magician, or comedian, Los Angeles has schools to help make them a reality!

Founded in 2009 by former Cirque du Soleil aerialist and Pickle Family Circus performer Aloysia Gavre and veteran theater, film, and TV producer Rex Camphuis, **Cirque School** (5640 1/2 Hollywood Blvd., 424/226-2477, www.cirqueschool.com) in Hollywood aims to make the circus arts more accessible to the general public, supported by its tagline: "anybody with any body." As someone who has been watching shows by the internationally renowned Cirque du Soleil for decades, the school instantly piqued my interest. It's for anyone who has ever imagined themselves dangling, twirling, and swinging in the air. When you first arrive and see students doing just that on the school's various apparatus, the question you may ask yourself (as I did) is, "Can I do *that*?" Cirque School's exhilarating indoor playground is equipped with hanging ropes, rows of trapeze bars, and streams of colorful, flowing fabrics. Although daunted, I was surprisingly—given my lack of a daily exercise regimen apart from casual walks—able to dangle from and strike poses on a trapeze during my first class, thanks to the support of my instructors and classmates. A willingness to try is everything. Cirque School offers four beginner classes: Acro-Fit 101 (overall strength building and rope work), Aerial 101 (trapeze and silks/fabric), Handstands 101, and Stretch 101. Each 60-minute class is broken into different segments to focus on training your body to use a specific apparatus and perform a series of tricks. Reserve classes (single class $30, discounts for 15-class pur-

▲ students on aerial silks at Cirque School

chase) in advance online. They're generally capped at eight students. If you take courses regularly, you'll also have the opportunity to participate in a recital, where you can show off and truly live out your circus dreams.

The Academy of Magical Arts was formed by attorney and magic enthusiast Will W. Larsen Sr. in 1951. It hosts classes in the exclusive and renowned **Magic Castle** (7001 Franklin Ave., 323/851-3313, www.magiccastle.com) overlooking Hollywood, a private Chateauesque clubhouse for magicians opened by Larsen's sons, Milt and Bill Jr. in 1963. Only members (including the likes of Penn & Teller, Larry Wilmore, Neil Patrick Harris, and Rob Zabrecky) and their invited guests, or those who've booked a room directly with the affiliated Magic Castle Hotel next door, can attend the clubhouse's daily magic shows—to which everyone in L.A. wants to score an invite. Fortunately, membership isn't required to enroll in the academy's popular six-week magic course ($350), which entails one two-hour class a week, with 12 students max. Students must be 21 and over. Start with Magic I to get an overview of the basics, including magic history and theory and introductory effects and techniques. You'll be given how-to handouts and a number of props, such as card decks, special coins, cups and balls, and, of course, a wand. In the classroom, students have their own tables and face the instructor, who guides them through how to perform different illusions. By the end of the six weeks, you'll be ready to do a few tricks at your next social gathering! My husband, who took the course, is proof of this. If you're hooked, you can retake the class to really hone those skills or continue with other classes in the series. A major perk of taking a class here is being granted the much sought-after entry to the clubhouse while enrolled. Take full advantage of this to see some of the most talented magicians in the world perform in different theaters in the multilevel space, or close up at magic tables, amid ornately decorated rooms featuring velvet galore and vintage magic posters and artifacts. My family is fans of Tokyo's Shoot Ogawa and Philadelphia's Eric Jones—both have appeared on the TV series *Penn & Teller: Fool Us* and *Masters of Illusion*—and Magic Castle instructors Kayla Drescher and friend Alfonso, who regularly perform in the clubhouse. There's a strict business/evening attire dress code for everyone who attends the clubhouse's shows as well as its classes.

The **Groundlings Theatre & School** (7284 Melrose Ave., 323/934-4747, http://groundlings.com) is an L.A. institution. It's part of our vocabulary: "Groundlings" is synonymous with comedy here. I can't even trace how it became part of mine—that's how engrained it is for locals. Maya Rudolph, Conan O'Brien, Jimmy Fallon, and Melissa McCarthy are alums. Founded by improv teacher Gary Austin in 1974, the Groundlings comedy troupe has been entertaining Angelenos for decades at its theater, where you'll typically see lines down the block for its improv and comedy sketch shows. The school offers Intro Track courses for students 18 and over with little or no acting or performing experience at its two-story brick building on Melrose Avenue across from the theater. A bonus is that students can attend Groundlings shows for free, and get access to half-price codes for additional tickets. Start with the one-session, three-hour Improv for Beginners ($45) to get acquainted with the Groundlings and basics of live improvisational theatre: working with partners and the "yes and" rule. The six-session, three-hour Improv Workshop A ($350) delves deeper into the fundamentals of the art form to help you develop your skills. Scholarships are available. Students who continue on and complete the next-level Core Track classes even get to perform on the Groundlings' main stage (dream realized!). Classes have 16 people max and fill up fast, so reserve your spot weeks in advance. Some tips for class: Be a good listener, make eye contact with your scene partner, embrace the unexpected, and have fun!

Sing along at Idle Hour's drag brunch

Entertainment and Events • Food and Drink

Why Go: Enjoy uplifting performances, delicious fare, and bottomless mimosas in an iconic space.

Where: 4824 Vineland Ave. • 818/980-5604 • www.idlehourbar.com • Metro bus 501 to Lankershim Blvd./Vineland Ave.

Timing: This 21-and-over event takes place one Saturday a month. Admission is free, but make a reservation at least a week in advance (www.bottomlessdrag. eventbrite.com). Doors open at 11am, and the two-hour show starts at 12:30pm. Arrive early to eat beforehand; you'll want to give the show your undivided attention.

North Hollywood's **Idle Hour** is a spectacle to behold—and that's even before its **Bottomless Drag Brunch** show starts. A Los Angeles Historic-Cultural Monument, the wooden wonder of a building is shaped like a giant whiskey barrel. Built in 1941, during the rise of car culture, the design was meant to lure motorists in for booze. Another example of this roadside attraction-like style known as programmatic architecture—which used to be prevalent around L.A.—sits on Idle Hour's patio: a giant pipe-smoking bulldog structure, a reproduction of the **Bulldog Café** eatery that opened in 1928 and closed in the '60s. Idle Hour today is a happening restaurant-bar and hosts one of the most energetic and tasty drag brunches in a city rife with them.

As you enter, you'll walk through the magnificent barrel and out onto the tree- and plant-bedecked courtyard where the show takes place. Seating options include standard tables with French seats, high tops with bar stools, and a bench around a central tree strewn with lights—and there's not a bad view in the house. A DJ spins tunes at club-level volumes before the show starts, perfect for getting the crowd excited (though you'll have to practically shout to have a conversation). Head chef Hannah Benage curates a special Drag Brunch menu that features bottomless mimosas and other cocktails, along with dishes ranging from blueberry-lemon cream puff pastries to crispy chicken and waffles with spicy maple syrup to

1: the Bulldog Café **2:** hostess Diana Dzhaketov with the author **3:** Taryn Balenciaga making her way through Idle Hour **4:** chicken and waffles

41

one of the best steaks I've had in recent memory (accompanied by chimichurri sauce, sunny-side-up eggs, and a side).

And then begins the no-holds-barred show, with performers emerging from the white bulldog. Bottomless Drag Brunch is hosted by the gorgeous and lovable Diana Dzhaketov, who kicks off the show and treats everyone like a friend, seemingly locking eyes with each of the 70-some diners. Dzhaketov is joined by a revolving cast of three other drag entertainers; on the day I went, it was Jordan Jayro, Salina EsTitties, and Taryn Balenciaga, with distinct looks and dance styles, performing three numbers each and working the tiled landing beneath the bulldog's large pipe to start. All made use of the picnic table at the foot of the stage to display their flexibility, as well as the poles of the patio awnings. Performances feature dramatic wardrobe changes, and the queens entertain in glorious color, from their wigs and makeup to their imaginative costumes and heels.

Be sure to have some cash on hand; your friendly servers can break large bills. As the performers work their way through the dollar-showering crowd, lip-syncing and dancing to

▴ Idle Hour's iconic exterior

More of L.A.'s Roadside-Attraction Architecture

Surviving programmatic architecture is rare in the city, but a few other spots besides Idle Hour are still standing: the 1938 camera-shaped storefront exterior of what was originally The Darkroom camera shop and is currently **Spare Tire Kitchen & Tavern** (5370 Wilshire Blvd.); the 1928 tamale-shaped building that was once, aptly, **The Tamale restaurant** (6421 Whittier Blvd.); and Hollywood celebrity hangout **Formosa Café** (7156 Santa Monica Blvd.), which originally opened in 1939—it incorporates one of L.A.'s original red trolley cars from 1904, visible from Formosa Avenue.

chosen tracks, a server follows them with a tip bucket. The playlist is as eclectic as the performers, from a Donna Summer medley and Whitney Houston's "All the Man That I Need" to Sixpence None the Richer's "Kiss Me" and Lizzo's "Good As Hell." Brilliantly edited music mixes feature dialogue and lyrics that allow the drag queens to highlight social injustices and provide group affirmations that get the whole crowd applauding.

The performers make it a point to engage everyone in the show and often get up close to patrons. Be prepared to have them take selfies or dance with/on you, interview you on the spot, urge you to down that mimosa while the crowd cheers you on, or possibly persuade you to take the stage to perform yourself. Our audience was a mix of people ranging from their 20s to 60s, including—this knowledge comes thanks to Dzhaketov's questioning during the show—a woman with friends celebrating her divorce, married entertainment industry couples, a group visiting from Sacramento, birthday celebrants, couples in love, and us four mamas taking a break from our kids. By the end of the show, we were all hoarse from endlessly cheering on the performers.

Connect with . . .

❾ See California's overlooked history at the *Great Wall of Los Angeles*

7 Find Griffith Park's hidden gems

Iconic L.A. • Get Outside • For All Ages

Why Go: Find a "wow" moment as you encounter something you never knew existed in L.A.'s most famous park.

Where: Griffith Park • 323/644-2050 • www.laparks.org/griffithpark • Metro B Line (Red) to Hollywood/Western or Metro bus 207 to Western/Franklin (Fern Dell), Metro bus 180 to Los Feliz/Commonwealth (Cedar Grove), Metro bus 96 to Griffith Park/Crystal Springs (Old Zoo) or L.A. Zoo (Wilson Harding Clubhouse)

Timing: Pick one spot for your day's adventure and plan on a few leisurely hours; these experiences shouldn't be rushed. While it's easy to pair a visit to the Old Zoo and clubhouse, the sites are otherwise spread out.

Each Angeleno has their favorite destinations in the 4,300-acre Griffith Park, which receives an estimated three million visitors each year. The **Griffith Observatory** is the most iconic, with its view of the Hollywood Sign and city, while locals prize the open green spaces and more than 50 miles of hiking trails. The park also includes attractions such as the **L.A. Zoo, Autry Museum of the American West, Greek Theatre,** and **Travel Town Museum.** But several smaller sights in Griffith Park are also deserving of attention.

One of the most enchanting but easy-to-miss sites in the park is **Fern Dell,** where a Gabrielino/Tongva village once was. It's a remarkable area of lushness in typically arid L.A.; my friend proposed to his now-wife here, which gives you a sense of what a magical urban oasis this is. Fern Dell is close to the park's southernmost entrance (Los Feliz Blvd. and Fern Dell Dr.); park along Fern Dell Drive, then walk up the block to Black Oak Drive to enter the Fern Dell gates. You'll be greeted with running streams and ponds and a foliage-lined dirt footpath including—yes—many types of ferns! A half-mile (one-way) trail through the natural area will take you north over and under small bridges, which were created in the 1930s by the Civilian Conservation Corps. You'll likely share the trail with couples sitting on benches lining the path, kids excitedly shrieking as they spot critters that inhabit the area (crayfish,

1: the caves of the Old Zoo **2:** Cedar Grove
3: Fern Dell **4:** the Wilson Harding Clubhouse

guppies, frogs, turtles), and people walking their dogs. At its terminus, you can stop at nearby locals' favorite food stand, **The Trails** (2333 Fern Dell Ave.)—our family always gets the avocado sandwich, snake dog (a hot dog in puff pastry), and lavender shortbread—or connect to trails that take you to the observatory (about a mile from here, one-way).

Another short walk we love takes you around the shady piece of forest paradise known as **Cedar Grove,** also on the park's southern end. A surprising oasis in the city, it has often been cast as a woodland backdrop in such films as *Twilight* and TV series including *Bones* and *Star Trek: The Next Generation.* There are various ways to access the grove—including an eponymous trail—but I prefer taking a circuitous route via paved roads for a more gradual ascent (better for kids and dogs) and great views along the way. Start at the park's Commonwealth Avenue entrance, where there's residential street parking, then bear left soon after onto Commonwealth Canyon Drive. Soon you'll come to a fork in the road; turn right onto Vista Del Valle Drive, which provides many breathtaking vantages of the city as it zigzags uphill en route to the grove's entrance—about a 15-minute walk from the fork—which is marked by a sign. You quickly feel dwarfed by the towering cedars. Hikers like resting on the oversized rocks at the grove's center, socializing on outlying benches, or sharing a meal at a picnic table. When you're ready, return the way you came or (if you're wearing shoes with good traction!) continue on the dirt trail along the periphery of the grove to complete a loop by following the shorter but much steeper 0.3-mile Cedar Grove Trail.

A unique feature in the park is the original site of the L.A. Zoo (1912-1966), known simply as the **Old Zoo.** It can be tricky to find since it's near the park's center and doesn't have an official address. I suggest entering via Crystal Springs Drive in the park's northeast corner, then turning left onto Griffith Park Drive; you'll pass Shane's Inspiration playground (4800 Crystal Springs Dr.) and take the first parking lot entrance to your left. Walk about five minutes southwest on the road and you'll see a paved path that winds up the hill. It leads to what's left of the Old Zoo, including remarkable faux hillside caves that used to be bear enclosures but now serve as a playground and fun photo backdrop. I've seen that "wow" expression on people's faces as they enter the caves—clearly for the first time—marveling at what looks like a Hollywood adventure movie set. Kids also enjoy role-playing in the steel-bar animal cages farther uphill. In summer, the month-long **Griffith Park Shakespeare**

Festival (818/710-6306, www.iscla.org, free) takes place on the grounds of the Old Zoo; kicking off in August, it features nightly performances of the bard's works.

From the Old Zoo, you can continue north on Griffith Park Drive for a short drive or 15-minute walk (watch for passing cars as there isn't a sidewalk) to the **Wilson Harding Clubhouse** (4730 Crystal Springs Dr., 323/661-7212) at the Wilson and Harding Golf Courses, where the likes of Tiger Woods and Babe Ruth have played. With its arched windows, terra-cotta-tiled roof, and restaurant with two outdoor dining areas with views of the adjoining courses and surrounding hillsides, the clubhouse is what draws this non-golfer here. You may have seen the beautiful, two-story Spanish Revival-style structure, built in 1937 by the Works Progress Administration, in period shows like *Mad Men*. It's also where my husband and I held our wedding reception. The grounds have the feel of a private country club without the snobbery, exclusionary policies, or membership fees. Grab a drink or order some of the clubhouse's solid fare, from breakfast burritos and pancakes to quesadillas and burgers. I love eating outdoors here and watching Angelenos of all ages and from all walks of life enjoying the public courses. The occasional L.A. Zoo tram passing along the grounds' periphery, with the tour guide and passengers' laughter in hearing distance, is a welcome addition to the soundscape. And don't be surprised to see a deer or coyote roaming the grounds—this is their playground too.

Connect with . . .

12 Take a walking tour of Los Feliz architecture
15 See stars at L.A. County's observatories
23 Bike along the L.A. River

Sample late-night tacos on Sunset Boulevard

Why Go: When a taco craving hits after a night out on the town, you'll find many tasty options along Sunset Boulevard to satisfy it.

Where: Sunset Blvd., between N. St. Andrews Pl. and Marion Ave. • Metro bus 2

Timing: These taco joints have closing times between 11pm and 3am on weekends.

Volumes can be written about tacos in L.A. I'm not here to share the best of the city (judge for yourself), but I am here to point out some of the prime spots along **Sunset Boulevard**— because nothing punctuates a good time out like a taco.

On the far eastern end of Sunset Boulevard is **Guisados** (1261 Sunset Blvd., 213/250-7600, www.guisados.la, 10am-10pm Mon.-Thurs., 9am-11pm Fri.-Sat., 9am-8pm Sun.), whose glowing neon signs always signal a tasty meal. Guisados opened its first location in 2010 and now has seven locations around L.A. Expect a line out the door at this Echo Park outpost. The chain's taco fillings are slow-cooked in homestyle stews (*guisados* in Spanish). Owner Armando De La Torre Sr. grew up eating his mom's preparations and, together with his son and co-owner, Armando De La Torre Jr., decided to serve *guisados* on handmade corn tortillas made with fresh masa rather than in a customary bowl. If you're really hungry or coming with a group, try the "OG" sampler of six different mini tacos, which includes *tinga de pollo* (shredded chicken cooked in a tomato-chipotle sauce), steak *picado* (chopped flank steak braised with bell peppers and bacon), and *chicarron* (pork rinds cooked in chile verde), among others. The chiles *toreados* (Thai chiles, serrano peppers, black beans with habanero sauce) is a noted vegetarian option. Lots of seating options are here, including an indoor dining room and a lighted patio with mural-decorated walls, but the prime seating for spectators is at the outside counter in front of the kitchen window.

Another good option, less than a mile west, is **Señor Fish** (1701 Sunset Blvd., 213/483-0161, http://señorfish.com, 10am-11:30pm daily), first opened in 1988 by siblings Enrique and

Leo's Tacos Truck in Hollywood

tacos by Tacos Kesly

bar seating in front of Guisados in Echo Park

Alicia Ramirez. It now has four locations, including this one in Echo Park. Its batter-fried fish tacos are my usual order, while my friends favor the scallop tacos and burritos. Be sure to check out the grilled fresh fish-of-the-day options, which may include mahi, swordfish, yellowtail, or sea bass. There are also crave-worthy breakfast tacos, overstuffed with bacon, eggs, and potatoes. Note that this is a popular destination for sports fans, with games playing on TVs by the bar, in the dining room, and on the large patio. The crowd gets animated, especially during playoffs!

Farther west and more convenient to Hollywood goings-ons is **Tacos Kesly** (5228 Sunset Blvd., 213/432-0251, 5pm-11pm Sun.-Thurs., 5pm-midnight Fri.-Sat., cash only), a sidewalk vendor in front of the 99 Cents Only store parking lot. Look for the pop-up tent and stainless-steel counter with rotating *al pastor* (pork) spit, large grill, and mega-sized pan of simmering chicken. *Lengua* (tongue) and *buche* (stomach) are also options. I love how multisensory this experience is: watching the heaps of meat and tortillas cooked up close—the *taqueros* mesmerizing as they work together in tandem behind the grill in what feels like a quick-paced, choreographed dance as they slice meat and flip tortillas—and breathing in aromas that heighten anticipation of that first bite. A long table full of toppings is set up for your indulgence, with cilantro, onions, cabbage, limes, cucumbers, sliced radishes, and several salsas (I particularly enjoy the habanero salsa). There's no seating here, so pop yourself on the curb or your car hood.

Leo's Tacos Truck (5525 Sunset Blvd., 323/346-2001, www.leostacostruck.com, 10am-2am Sun.-Thurs., 10am-3am Fri.-Sat., cash only) started in 2010 and has seven locations around L.A, including this one a few blocks west of Tacos Kesly in the WSS shoe store parking lot, which draws a sizable crowd. Leo's brightly colored truck—bearing the brand's familiar mustached man giving a thumbs-up—is a traffic-stopper, lined with lights and a flashing LED sign announcing "Tacos." Of the spots on this list, Leo's is open the latest and is the cheapest, starting at $1.25 a taco. The truck is most famous for its *al pastor,* which comes topped with a slice of pineapple. I'd happily eat three back-to-back. Leo's also has the usual carnivorous options such as chorizo and carnitas, as well as one uncommon offering: *tripas* (beef tripe). Request the toppings and salsas you'd like. There are tables and chairs set up

Taco-Tasting Tips

If you're so inclined, you could bike, bus, or drive your way down Sunset and sample a taco at each of the spots covered here. Or if you don't have the stomach space for all of them, note that Guisados and Señor Fish are a two-minute drive apart in Echo Park, while Tacos Kesly and Leo's are just a three-minute drive apart in Hollywood—so it'd be easy no matter which spot you choose to hop to a second if you want to indulge in a comparison tasting. While you can walk between these destinations, most of the storefronts along these stretches are closed late at night.

My go-to neighborhood taco place by day is the lovable Los Feliz shack **Yuca's** (2056 Hillhurst Ave., 323/662-1214, www.yucasla.com, 11am-6pm Mon.-Sat.), a James Beard Award recipient in the America's Classics category. My friend Dora Herrera, president of Yuca's Restaurants, has, as you can imagine, some taco know-how and has accompanied me on some of my taco-eating adventures. Dora suggests, when embarking on a taco crawl, that you order the same tacos at each place to compare the cook's touch on a dish. A tip from her mom, "Mama" Socorro Herrera: Take your first taco bite without adding anything, to savor the flavor of the meat(s).

in the lot for you to enjoy your tacos, and this is a fun spot for people-watching the eclectic Hollywood crowd end a night out.

Connect with . . .

18 Go on a bar crawl at Hollywood hotels

See California's overlooked history at the *Great Wall of Los Angeles*

Iconic L.A. • Art and Culture

Why Go: This magnificent half-mile mural highlights significant local events and leaders too often ignored in history books.

Where: Along the west flood channel wall parallel to Coldwater Canyon Ave. between Burbank Blvd. and Oxnard St. in Valley Glen • Metro bus 167 and 237 or Van Nuys/Studio City DASH to Burbank Blvd./Coldwater Canyon

Timing: Allow a couple of hours on a first visit to walk alongside and contemplate this expansive mural.

In L.A., some of our most priceless artifacts are not housed in a museum or encased in glass but situated in public spaces accessible to all; the cement walls along the city's waterways have long been (unsanctioned) canvases for artists. But nothing can compare to the **Great Wall of Los Angeles** in terms of sheer size—it's 2,754 feet long—and breadth of historical coverage. One of the greatest artworks and cultural treasures in Los Angeles, it runs along the flood channel wall of the Tujunga Wash deep in the San Fernando Valley. The mural was spearheaded by Chicana artist and activist Judy Baca in collaboration with the **Social and Public Art Resource Center** (SPARC, http://sparcinla.org), which she cofounded and where she serves as artistic director. Originally named "The History of California," it focuses on telling the stories of peoples who have been historically underrepresented and marginalized in the state—including women as well as BIPOC and LGBTQA people.

Rendered in the artistic style of the 1920s and '30s Mexican muralists—large scale and politically themed—the wall is composed of 86 titled segments. Baca designed the majority of them, with Kristi Lucas, Christina Schlesinger, Judith Hernandez, Ulysses Jenkins, Gary Takamoto, Arnold Ramirez, Olga Muniz, Charlie Brown, and Isabel Castro also contributing to segment designs. More than 400 community members, including youths and their families, joined Baca and other artists to create the mural in 1974 and the subsequent summers of 1978, 1980, 1981, and 1983. Created by so many individuals, the *Great Wall of Los Angeles*

▲ *Great Wall of Los Angeles*

▲ overlooked events involving Chinese immigrants in California and L.A. history

is an illustrated history that every Californian should view. There is palpable drama in every colorful vignette, in each facial expression and landscape depicted.

Because of its location in the Tujunga Wash, below street level, passing cars aren't likely to glimpse it as they zoom past. You need to be on foot to properly view it; there is plenty of street parking along Coldwater Canyon if you come by car. Start at the corner of Burbank and Coldwater Canyon to see it in chronological order, beginning with the **"Pre-Historic California, 20,000 B.C."** segment, featuring a giant sloth, flying vulture, and saber-toothed cat against a hilly landscape. This corner offers the only unhindered view of the mural's grandeur; for the rest of the way, you'll only be able to view the wall through a chain-link fence. Head north on the path cutting through the narrow lawn dotted with trees that runs along the flood channel's fenceline and the length of the mural. The mural currently ends at Oxnard Street with **"Olympic Champions: Breaking Barriers, 1964-1984,"** including portraits of diver Sammy Lee, sprinter Wilma Rudolph, and track-and-field star Billy Mills.

There are many images of the mural in books and documentaries, but it's a work that

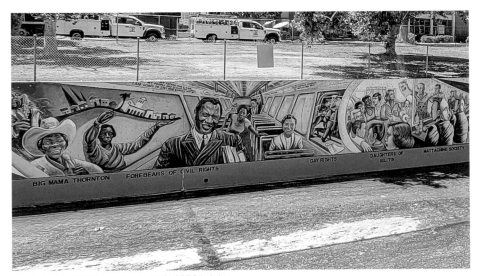

▲ pioneers in music, civil rights, and LGBTQA rights

needs to be seen in person to fully appreciate the achievements, obstacles, and, often, trage-dies that many communities of color have faced in our city and state. Had I visited earlier—if it were required "reading" in schools—I would've learned about many pivotal events and organizations that I only became acquainted with in recent years: the 1871 massacre of Chinese immigrants in Los Angeles; the 1943 Zoot Suit Riots in L.A. during which U.S. service-men targeted Mexican American and other minority males; and early lesbian and gay activist groups Daughters of Bilitis and Mattachine Society. Note that some imagery depicts human suffering, including lynchings and the forced assimilation of Indigenous communities. The mural also celebrates many trailblazing individuals, such as singer and songwriter Big Mama Thornton, entrepreneur and activist Biddy Mason, and labor organizer Luisa Moreno. I'll be visiting the mural again to take in more history and bring my young daughter.

The *Great Wall of Los Angeles* is a work in progress. SPARC plans to expand the mural to include events up to 2020, and other future additions include an "interpretative green bridge," a cement bridge over the flood channel for better viewing of the mural, with both sides of the bridge surrounded by green landscaping and no fence in sight.

Connect with . . .

🔟 Revel in L.A. car culture at Van Nuys Cruise Night
⓳ Ride a swan boat (Lake Balboa)

10 Revel in L.A. car culture at Van Nuys Cruise Night

Iconic L.A. • *Entertainment and Events* • *Neighborhoods and City Streets*

Why Go: It's a SoCal tradition to cruise the boulevard and show off your vintage or tricked-out car, and drivers have plenty of space to flaunt their wheels on Van Nuys Cruise Night.

Where: Van Nuys Blvd. in Van Nuys, often between Sherman Way and Vanowen St. or Oxnard St. and Burbank Blvd. • Metro bus 233 to Van Nuys/Vose

Timing: Cruise Night generally takes place on select Saturdays 5pm-11pm but can occur other days of the week as well. Follow @vannuysblvdcruisenight on Instagram, which posts about upcoming events on the street.

Custom car culture is cherished in L.A., and nothing brings the drama quite like the low-riders, bouncing down the boulevard, announcing themselves with style and spectacle—the lowrider scene was born here, after all. Beginning in the 1940s and '50s, Mexican Americans returning from World War II started customizing their rides using mechanical skills they learned in the military to highlight their culture or individual style and express their opposition to the status quo. Instead of accepting U.S. car models (and ideals, you could say) as they were, these trailblazers lowered and imaginatively painted their cars in vibrant shades, often incorporating cultural and religious imagery, with showy interiors to match. They also rebuilt or customized old models, and instead of embracing speed, drove them low and slow—and even made them dance, using hydraulics. An integral part of this scene was, and still is, the camaraderie of the lowrider community—taking pride in what you built yourself versus bought ready-made.

Coming upon a nighttime cruise event on a city street feels like a special happening, with the sounds of engines as cars crawl down the asphalt, taillights and brake lights illuminating the boulevard, and drivers with their windows rolled down—an arm hanging over the door, another on the wheel, and soundtrack blasting. But you don't need to leave this experience to chance; **Van Nuys Cruise Night** in the San Fernando Valley takes place

▲ Lo Low's Car Club Southern Califas sign

▲ "Spanish Rose" motorcycle by Techniques East L.A.

▲ two Chevrolets from Old Memories Car Club

▲ Stylistics member Isaac Torres and his Impala

on a semi-regular basis, bringing energy and excitement. The boulevard offers a nice, wide stretch of playground for cars and fans alike, with four lanes, plenty of parking on both sides of the street, spacious sidewalks for hanging out and admiring from the sidelines, and street vendors selling food including tacos, pretzels, and hot dogs (plus a cool dessert trailer serving crepes and churros).

Van Nuys Boulevard has a long history, starting in the '50s, as a popular cruising street, but in the early '80s, local authorities started blocking off streets to prevent cruising nights, citing street racing, traffic jams, and rowdy crowds. Around 2010, Van Nuys Cruise Night returned thanks to open communication between organizers and LAPD about upcoming events, as well as hosting car clubs ensuring the area is cleaned up afterward. Today, neighborhood residents and local police welcome the events as long as participants and spectators keep the streets tidy and leave the drama to the cars.

Different car clubs and individuals can initiate a cruise. I once went with some girlfriends on August 18, "818 Cruise Night"; the date matches the Valley's area code and is known as Valley Day, or 818 Day. Lo Low's Car Club Southern Califas, founded in 1997, hosted the evening (big shout-out to Lo Low's president Jimmy Martinez and "First Lady" Eunice for welcoming us with open arms). It has chapters all over California, as well as in Texas and Pennsylvania, and the club's members drive mostly luxury late-model cars, especially those manufactured in the 1990s.

Members of car clubs—including Van Nuys Cruisers, Firme Bombs, Primeros, StreetWise, Stylistics, and Techniques, as well as Lo Low's—cruise or cluster along the boulevard (look for signs in the backs of cars to identify the clubs), while people sit in lawn chairs on the sidewalks and watch the action. Drive your own wheels (all wheels welcome, as they say) or come just to spectate as you would at any parade.

It's thrilling to see Chevrolet Monte Carlos and Impalas, Cadillacs, and Oldsmobiles galore drive by, especially when equipped with hydraulic systems or sliding by on two or three wheels to the beat of the driver's favorite track. You'll overhear some "whoas," maybe elicited by an-out-of-town club member's car, a solo rider's rare vintage car restored to its original 1930s glory, or a lime-green Lincoln Town Car featuring a purple-outlined mini mural of women's faces cruising by with its left wheels suspended in the air (yeah, I saw that at a Van Nuys Cruise Night).

Parked cars at cruise scenes—along with other vehicles, including bicycles and motorcycles, maybe even a minivan elaborately decorated in cool fashion—are meant to be admired, so check them out up close and chat up the owners about their wheels. We met Isaac Torres of Stylistics CC San Fernando Valley. The Stylistics started in 1996 in South L.A. and now has chapters in Texas, Arizona, and San Diego, as well as Japan. Torres's ride is a 1969 two-door Impala painted in "candy" brandywine and metal-flake with ghost-pearl patterns and gold-leaf pinstriping. The car was his godmother's, and he rode around in it as a kid, then saved up his money so he could buy it from her when he was older. "My family has always had lowriders. It's a way of life," he said. "Lowriding was a way for the family to get out and just have some fun out on the streets without doing anything wrong. It's been in my blood."

Other cruising destinations around the city include **Whittier Boulevard** in East L.A. (considered the heart of the SoCal scene); **Stadium Way** in Elysian Park, home of Dodgers Stadium (the Dodgers even have a lowrider cheer graphic that plays during its games to get the fans excited); **York Boulevard** in Highland Park; and **Brand Park** in Mission Hills.

Follow @la_cruisenights_carshows and @los.angeles.lowrider.community on Instagram for upcoming rides in the city.

Connect with . . .

9 See California's overlooked history at the *Great Wall of Los Angeles*

11 Watch movies in historic theaters

Iconic L.A. • Entertainment and Events • Art and Culture

Why Go: In the epicenter of the U.S. film industry, our oldest cinemas are as revered as the medium itself.

Where: Citywide

Timing: Check theater websites for schedules and special events.

In an era of chain multiplexes, Los Angeles is lucky enough to have held onto some of its single-screen movie palaces, constructed during the golden age of cinema and among the city's architectural treasures. I can't imagine the city without its vintage movie houses; these marvelous holdouts from another era hold indelible memories for generations of film lovers as the places where they lined up patiently (and impatiently), ate too much popcorn, had first and last dates, and cheered or jeered at endings. Today, audiences at these beloved historic theaters are treated to unique moviegoing experiences; this is where the Hollywood dream factory is based, after all. To boot, you may spot the occasional celebrity in the crowd and enjoy the curious phenomenon of people actually staying for the end credits and applauding; folks in the audience often worked on the films themselves.

Hard-core indie film fans across Southern California have long ventured to the **New Beverly Cinema** (7165 Beverly Blvd., 323/938-4038, http://thenewbev.com) since it opened in 1929. During college, my friends and I were among them, making the trek to the Fairfax neighborhood from Orange County several times a month, eager to pick up the monthly calendar—typically featuring international, arthouse, and cult releases playing nowhere else—and proudly taping it to our fridges to determine our social lives. Back then, in the early '90s, I recall being mesmerized by Katsuhiro Otomo's *Akira,* surrendering daylight in exchange for a double feature of Jean-Pierre Jeunet and Marc Caro's *Delicatessen* and Terry Gilliam's *Brazil,* and flinching during the ear scene at a packed midnight screening of Quentin Tarantino's *Reservoir Dogs*. Who knew that many years later Tarantino would own

1: New Beverly Cinema 2: El Capitan Theatre
3: TCL Chinese Theatre 4: Vista Theatre

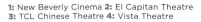

the theater and, thankfully, preserve its most treasured offerings: the coolest L.A. movie theater calendar ever, double features, midnight screenings of his films, and 35mm projection. The filmmaker largely determines the programming at the theater, sharing prints from his vast collection, which is as eclectic as New Beverly fans. Families also appreciate his addition of Kiddee Matinees, during which kids 12 and under receive free popcorn.

In 2021, Tarantino also purchased my favorite theater of all time: Los Feliz's **Vista Theatre** (4473 Sunset Blvd., 323/660-6639, www.vintagecinemas.com/vista), which opened in 1923. Locals are often as excited to see beloved theater manager Victor Martinez—greeting guests while dressed as one of the featured film characters—as they are a movie at this venue. The theater's Egyptian-inspired interiors are stunning, as is the lovingly preserved ticket booth. The Vista also has its own collection of celebrity foot- and handprints. Filmgoers can look forward to a mix of new and old movies projected on film.

Two of the most well-known movie palaces in the world are on the **Hollywood Walk of Fame.** Seeing a movie at Grauman's Chinese Theatre, now known as the **TCL Chinese Theatre** (6925 Hollywood Blvd., 323/461-3331, www.tclchinesetheatres.com), which opened in 1927, is a must, with its dramatically designed exterior, including a stone-carved dragon framed by two red columns and a towering pagoda-shaped roof. It is *the* most popular theater for red-carpet premieres and is indeed a tourist trap, but the wide-eyed international crowd is part of the spectacle. The theater's Forecourt of the Stars—marked by celebrity hand- and footprints—leads to the entrance doors. And if you think the themed architecture is cool on the outside, wait until you walk inside. A magnificent eyeful awaits visitors, from the lobby murals and light fixtures to every wood-carved inch of the auditorium's incredible ceiling. And the theater's film projection and sound quality are superior, too. Settle into a classic red velvet seat to enjoy a Hollywood blockbuster in an immersive IMAX environment on one of the largest screens (a curved one, at that) in the city.

Across the street at the Spanish Colonial-style **El Capitan Theatre** (6638 Hollywood Blvd., 818/845-3110, http://elcapitantheatre.com), which dates to 1926, there's always an added element of surprise to the moviegoing experience. This may include exhibits of props and costumes from the featured film, live performances before the movie starts—during which the Wurlitzer organ often steals the show—and/or 4D effects (indoor snow, anyone?).

Hollywood Boulevard's Big Night

Hollywood rolls out the biggest red carpet of the year along the boulevard between the El Capitan and TCL Chinese Theatres when it hosts the annual **Hollywood Christmas Parade** (http://thehollywoodchristmasparade.org, first Sunday after Thanksgiving), beloved by families. First held in 1928, the nighttime parade covers about three miles and features themed floats, towering balloon characters from pop culture, and school and cultural group performances. Celebrities also take part, riding in cars along the boulevard, which is gloriously lit during the holiday season; recent hosts and guests have included Danny Trejo, Montel Williams, Erik Estrada, and Marilyn McCoo. Ride the Metro to get there and bring your good cheer!

Owned by Disney, the El Capitan screens new Disney and Marvel films and is often the site of their world premieres. It also shows classics from the Disney Vault and much-loved seasonal repeats, such as Tim Burton's *Nightmare Before Christmas*. The balcony seats offer an especially awesome vantage; from here you can see the dramatically lit stage and luxurious curtains beneath the ornate wonder of an arched ceiling. As the curtains are drawn and the music starts, it feels like a grand event even before a single frame is shown.

The 1929 **Nuart Theatre** (11272 Santa Monica Blvd., 310/472-8530, www.landmarktheatres.com) on the Westside is another L.A. essential. The art deco theater is a popular destination for its international and arthouse programming, along with its slate of new releases—with directors and actors often appearing to present their films. But it's the Saturday midnight screening of *The Rocky Horror Picture Show* that is the must-see here, especially if you're a virgin viewer of the 1975 horror/comedy/musical cult classic. The experience starts before you enter the theater, with Sins O' The Flesh, the Nuart's longtime accompanying performance troupe, often appearing in character, while fans—some also dressed as their favorite characters—line up beneath the theater's neon marquee. Once inside the Nuart's more modern interiors, expect people dancing about before the film starts. Over the course of the movie, join the chorus of audience chants as the live cast performs in front of the screen and in the aisles. The atmosphere is boisterous and the performances graphic. If you lose your voice after actively participating, you've done it right.

12 Take a walking tour of Los Feliz architecture

Neighborhoods and City Streets • Art and Culture • Get Outside

Why Go: The hills are alive with notable residences in a range of styles by a who's who of L.A. architects.

Where: Los Feliz • Metro bus 180 to Los Feliz/Commonwealth

Timing: Budget at least an hour for this approximately 2.5-mile round-trip walk. Street parking is readily available near the starting point outside of weekday rush hours.

Los Feliz features some of the most eclectic, iconic, and expensive residential architecture in the city, especially on the hillside below the most famous building in L.A., the Griffith Observatory. Here you'll find many local landmarks designated by the city of Los Angeles as Historic-Cultural Monuments, from homes by renowned architects to municipal staircases to the deodar cedar trees that line Los Feliz Boulevard. I've called this neighborhood home for nearly three decades, and this is one of my favorite walks. Wear comfortable shoes and bring a water bottle, as you'll be climbing steep staircases and going up and down hills.

Start your tour at the northwest corner of Los Feliz Boulevard and Commonwealth Avenue with a large helping of midcentury architecture: the 14-story **Los Feliz Towers** (4455 Los Feliz Blvd.), a pair of 1966 high-rises—the only ones in Los Feliz—designed by the DMJM firm. Whether you consider them eyesores or not, they are among the most recognizable buildings in the neighborhood.

Head west on Los Feliz Boulevard to see the 1927 art deco beauty known as the **Los Feliz Manor** (4363 Los Feliz Blvd., www.losfelizmanor.com), originally a hotel and now apartments. Peek through its doors to see the wonderfully preserved lobby and elevator. As you continue walking west, look up to get a view of its rooftop. Look familiar? Key scenes from the 1994 Beastie Boys' "Sabotage" music video, directed by Spike Jonze, were shot there.

Cross Vermont Avenue, then proceed north on it for a block to arrive at the decorative

Los Feliz Heights Steps

Lee McVetta mural along public starcase off Bonvue Avenue

Ennis House

Blackburn Residence

wrought-iron gate of a 1926 **Tudor Revival brick mansion** (2405 Glendower Ave.), which formerly housed the Russian consulate and was designed by Harold S. Johnson, one of the architects of Downtown's Beaux Arts L.A. Railway Building. From here, head west on Cromwell Avenue, pausing to take your picture against the lengthy brick wall of the estate, which makes a great backdrop. Next up is the 1923 Colonial Revival-style **Welfer Residence** (4784 Cromwell Ave.), designed by A. F. Leicht, one of the architects of Echo Park's Angelus Temple. Soon after is the 1927 Spanish Colonial Revival-style **Blackburn Residence** (4791 Cromwell Ave.) by the legendary Paul Revere Williams, who designed the LAX Theme Building, parts of the Beverly Hills Hotel, and almost 2,000 L.A. residences.

Just past the neighboring house to the west, take the **Los Feliz Heights Steps** (aka **Berendo Stairs**), a municipal staircase with a decorative concrete entrance featuring a lion's head at its center. It's a steep climb that locals often work out on for good reason: There are 181 steps! You can take a breather at the bougainvillea-covered landing, which has seating, about halfway up. At the top, you'll arrive at Bonvue Avenue. Follow Bonvue east (right) up the hill until you see a sign indicating a set of staircases that will shortcut you to the upper part of Glendower. The first staircase (79 steps) winds you around a mosaic mural of the Griffith Observatory and Hollywood Sign, installed in 2020 by Venice Community Housing youth on a wall that was previously covered in graffiti. The stairs end on the Bryn Mawr Road cul-de-sac, in view of the next staircase (133 steps); on your way up, turn around for a spectacular city view.

Turn right on Glendower to begin a small clockwise loop and gawk at the many multimillion-dollar houses along it. The most famous house on the hillside is Frank Lloyd Wright's magnificent Mayan Revival **Ennis House** (2655 Glendower Ave., http://franklloydwright.org), completed in 1924 and composed of textile blocks (like his Hollyhock House, a UNESCO World Heritage Site)—more than 27,000 in all. Its exterior featured heavily as the house in the Vincent Price classic *House on Haunted Hill* (1959), and scenes from other movies like *Blade Runner* and *Mulholland Drive* and the TV series *Buffy the Vampire Slayer* were shot here. Listen for the large wind chimes in the neighboring trees that make the scene even more magical (thanks to whoever added these!).

Across the street from the Ennis House is another Leicht-designed home, the 1924

Barnsdall Art Park

Barnsdall Art Park (4800 Hollywood Blvd., 323/660-4254, www.barnsdall.org) is home to the Frank Lloyd Wright-designed **Hollyhock House** (http://hollyhockhouse. org, prices vary), a treasured architectural landmark not to be missed. Here you can also see works by local artists at the **Los Angeles Municipal Art Gallery** (www.lamag. org, free). Then join locals socializing on the park's hillside lawn—with dreamy views (especially at sunset) of the Hollywood Sign and the palm-tree-dotted neighborhoods below.

John Philip Law House (2600 Glendower Ave.), or the "Castle" as it's known. Icons of the music and art worlds have stayed here: Bob Dylan, The Beatles, Andy Warhol, and the Velvet Underground. It was also once owned by a member of the Getty family. Many influences—including Assyrian, Spanish, and Moderne styles—played into its design. Note the round tower room on top, where Nico once lived and composed songs.

A quick walk farther brings you to the 1923 Storybook-style **Hlaffer-Courcier Residence** (2574 Glendower Ave.), aka the "Witches' Whimsy," as signage on its gate reads, designed and built by Rufus Beck.

Your last stop is where Glendower meets the east entrance of Bryn Mawr Road, the 1952 Modernist **Skolnik House** (2567 Glendower Ave.) by famed Vienna-born architect R. M. Schindler, who worked for Frank Lloyd Wright, oversaw the construction of the Hollyhock House, and became influential in SoCal residential architecture in his own right. Known for what he termed "space architecture," his innovative structures were often built on challenging sites, like this hilltop, and designed to maximize the flow of natural light indoors. You'll want to walk up Bryn Mawr to get a better look at the multiangled home.

To head back, continue down Glendower, veering left—just before the set of stairs you took previously—to stay on the street (note there aren't any sidewalks on a quarter-mile stretch) until you hit Vermont Avenue, which you'll follow back to Los Feliz Boulevard. If your timing is right, you might luck into the fruit cart at the gas station on the corner of Vermont and Los Feliz for a cool pick-me-up—order with chile seasoning, *chamoy* (pickled fruit) sauce, and lime juice!—before heading east back to the starting point at Commonwealth.

Buy fresh blooms in the Flower District

Neighborhoods and City Streets • Shopping

Why Go: Find a floral high at the largest wholesale flower district in the country.

Where: Downtown, district bordered by Wall St. and San Pedro St., E. 7th St. and E. 9th St. • Metro bus 66 to 8th/San Julian or 51 to San Pedro/8th

Timing: Come in the morning to experience the bustle of the largest markets (except on Sundays, when they're closed), then spend the afternoon roaming the district's smaller-yet-mighty stores, which stay open into the evening.

Visiting the **Los Angeles Flower District** (http://laflowerdistrict.com) for the first time is an exciting (albeit potentially overwhelming) experience, with approximately 200 wholesale and retail vendors spanning six blocks. People venture here for the vast floral selection, sourced from all over the world, and especially the friendly prices; this is a destination for those shopping for special occasions, from baptisms to funerals, marriage proposals to anniversaries (all my wedding flowers and decorations came from the district). But it's also fun to visit without an agenda; I've spent mornings at these highly trafficked marketplaces just to enjoy the rush of energy and people-watching and browse the array of flowers. You'll experience the celebratory-to-somber spectrum of floral creations at every turn, with blooms sold in imaginative arrangements or whatever form you can dream up.

Start with the largest indoor marketplaces (both of which open to wholesalers before dawn and to the public as early as 6am, generally closing by noon), specifically the mart that gave birth to the L.A. Flower District: the **Southern California Flower Market** (742 Maple Ave., 213/627-2482, www.socalflowermarket.com, $1-2 admission), which was founded by Japanese American growers in 1909. The two-story building features around 40 vendors and also has an event space where floral instructors occasionally offer workshops. Visit **Yamaoka Flowers** (stall #22) for lilies, dahlias, and anemones and **Divine Orchids & More** (stall #25) for tropical flowers and leis. Next, head across the street from the mart's Wall

an arrangement at La Esquina del Amor

Junior, "Mayor of the Flower District"

blooms at the Original Los Angeles Flower Market

Street exit to the **Original Los Angeles Flower Market** (754 Wall St., 213/627-3696, originallaflowermarket.com, $1-2 admission), founded in 1919 by European American growers and home to 50 vendors boasting well over 100 varieties of cut flowers. **Wall Street Floral** (stall #20) has been in operation since the 1920s and has playful offerings such as colored baby's breath and rainbow roses, while **Flores Deos Co.** (stall #7b) offers tuberoses, birds of paradise, and alstroemerias.

Just south, the **California Flower Mall** (825 San Pedro St., 213/488-1983, http://californiaflowermall.com, free admission) houses 30 family-owned businesses, organized into separate stalls that are easily navigable via a central aisle (versus the mazelike—but fun to explore!—layouts of its neighboring marketplaces).

For ready-made arrangements, potted plants, and other finds, visit some of the smaller shops on the surrounding streets; come after 2pm for a mellower shopping experience. Highly curated and spacious showroom **Moon Atelier** (817 San Pedro St. #C and 822 San Julian St., 213/627-0808, www.moonatelierla.com) inspires patrons with its staged living spaces featuring plants and decor for sale. A couple of blocks southwest, **La Esquina del Amor** (800 S. San Pedro St., 323/671-8511) showcases large-scale, sculptured centerpieces featuring roses. About a block north, on the corner of San Julian and 8th Streets, longtime Angelenos should be sure to look up to see neon signage from the once-happening, 1980s-era Gorky's Cafe and Russian Brewery (ah, I miss that 24-hour joint), now home to **Event Supplier Wholesale & Retail Distributor Inc.** (536 E. 8th St., 213/327-0551), where you'll find walls blanketed in bouquets of artificial flowers and long vines, perfect photo backdrops.

Some tips: It's not a bad idea to come to the Flower District with a wish list if you're on a hunt. If you won't be returning home right away with your purchases and it's a hot day, bring a large pitcher or pail to store your flowers, or a spray bottle to spritz your plants. Paid parking lots as well as metered parking can be found around the L.A. Flower District.

If you get hungry, convenient options include neighborhood favorite **Poppy + Rose** (765 Wall St., 213/995-7799, www.poppyandrosela.com) in the Southern California Flower Market (stall #8), with a menu including shrimp and grits, a fried chicken waffle sandwich, and pulled pork hash, and **QQ Cafe** (824 San Julian St., Unit 16, 213/624-0860, www.qq-cafetogo.com), in California Flower Mall's central courtyard, where you can enjoy a variety

The Cats of the L.A. Flower District

During the district's busiest hours, you may not notice them amid the crowds, but later in afternoon, it's easier to spot them: the cats of the L.A. Flower District. Like many local indie bookstores, shops in the Flower District commonly have feline residents. "Everyone has one," said one vendor, smiling. They serve as companions, help lure customers into shops, and repel rodents that damage precious inventory. I caught gray-and-white Concha napping atop a display one day, after which more felines came out to play, happily greeting passersby with meows, looking for friendly rubs, with locals calling each out by name. The cat that stole my heart was a one-eared, tough-looking black cat named Junior, who carries himself like he is the mayor of the Flower District. Junior enjoys belly rubs and lives and lounges on the counter at **California Flowers** (506 W. 8th St. B, 213/622-3452, www.lacaliforniaflowers.com), known for its floral boxes as well as its many other cats—Garfield, Mami, Princessa—and their canine friend, Coco. Paola Eliza Gamez, whose family owns the store, is a longtime animal rescuer. She says that sometimes neighborhood strays come to her, or she brings them from elsewhere, and clients end up adopting them. Drop by for a beautiful bouquet and, perhaps, a new furry friend.

of dishes, from pancakes and omelets to menudos and fajitas. The **Piñata District,** just a 15-minute walk south, also has a number of delicious Latin American street food options.

Connect with . . .

26 Enjoy the cultural feast of the Piñata District
28 Eat your way around Asia at specialty markets (Little Tokyo Market Place)
39 Browse antique and architectural salvage stores

14 Get your photo taken by a local legend

Iconic L.A. • Art and Culture

Why Go: Photographer Gary Leonard has captured L.A. life like no other for decades—and getting one's picture taken by him is on many Angelenos' bucket lists.

Where: Citywide

Timing: Look out for Leonard throughout the year roaming city sidewalks and rooftops and at L.A.'s biggest and most unique cultural events.

If you live in Los Angeles long enough, you'll become familiar with a handful of local celebrities who are integral to the city's fabric; spotting them out and about is akin to a *Where's Waldo?* adventure that never gets old. Among them is **Gary Leonard** (www.takemypicture.com), an award-winning photographer who has been documenting the city since he was a child, starting in 1960. Leonard shared that he sees his photography as "kind of a personal, postwar chronicle. As a native Angeleno, I'm kind of inspired by what I know and where I come from."

I was first introduced to his work in the early '90s through **"Take My Picture, Gary Leonard,"** a regular column that ran in the *Los Angeles Reader* until it ceased publication in 1996. It always featured a single black-and-white photo, dated and signed with a short caption. Each Thursday I looked forward to picking up the latest issue of the free weekly to see who was lucky enough to be snapped by him, and where. Leonard served as our unofficial tour guide to the city and its myriad iconic (or soon to be) sites, as he captured many of today's landmarks under construction and those responsible for them, from the people building them to city leaders. Selected photos were published in a *Take My Picture Gary Leonard* book in 1999, and the column later ran, through 2020, with color photos on the **LA Observed website** (www.laobserved.com). Now fans don't need to wait a week to see his photos; you can get a daily helping of archival and current shots on his **Instagram profile (@tmpgaryleonard).**

1: *Traffic control officers in the Crenshaw District,* January 1994. Photo by Gary Leonard. **2:** Gary Leonard sighting in Los Feliz **3:** iron workers who put the spire on the Wilshire Grand in Downtown L.A. in 2016. Photo by Gary Leonard.

writer Andrea Richards, photographer Gary Leonard, and author Teena Apeles in front of sculpture by Charlie Becker at LACE

Sure, there are photos of well-known L.A. folks from the art world, politics, and sports, but what most locals treasure (then and now) are the images of everyday Angelenos who, through Leonard's thoughtful lens, are elevated to celebrity status. From joyful portraits of female traffic officers on break in the Crenshaw District to fedora-wearing teenagers on low-rider bikes in the Echo Park Christmas parade, he captures the L.A. we know or want to know.

To be one of Leonard's subjects has been a goal for generations of Angelenos. While you could just hire him to take your portrait, where's the thrill in that? After nearly two decades of running into him at various sites and events around the city (and having my photo taken by him on a handful of occasions, usually with my camera turned on him as well), I have some tips for spotting him.

First, commit to memory his short gray hair and friendly face (often sporting a groomed beard) as well as telltale cameras (typically one strapped across his body and one in hand). Next, explore the city the way he does: appreciating everyday slices of life at, say, neighborhood bus stops or skyline-changing construction sites, as well as seeking out newsworthy events like the **L.A. Marathon** and **CicLAvia.** I've also run into him over the years at major happenings at **Griffith Park** and **Chinatown Summer Nights.**

It's also fun to do a little research. The Los Angeles Public Library (http://tessa.lapl.org) features more than 2,500 of his photos, dating back to 1972, in its digital collections. Study the people he's chronicled and note the sites visited, like **Philippe's restaurant** (1001 N. Alameda St., 213/628-3781, www.philippes.com) and **Skylight Books** (1818 N. Vermont Ave., 323/660-1175, www.skylightbooks.com). He's known to still revisit these spots.

In the age of social media, you also have an advantage that we didn't in earlier days; you can follow him on Instagram to see what parts of town he's currently frequenting.

Put yourself out there and you may find him. As far as how to approach him, Leonard suggests, "Talk to me, we'll have a conversation." Hopefully he'll turn his camera on you before you even have to say, "Take my picture, Gary Leonard." If you're fortunate enough to become one of his subjects, will you ever see the photo? "Remember the date I take it," says the photographer. "I'll always be able to recall and get it to you."

Connect with . . .

① Cycle down car-free streets during CicLAvia

④ Dance under the stars at Chinatown Summer Nights

15 See stars at L.A. County's observatories

Iconic L.A. • For All Ages

Why Go: Gaze into the night sky, take in panoramic views, and learn more about the cosmos at these stellar observatories.

Where: Griffith Observatory, Los Feliz, LADOT Observatory DASH bus to Griffith • Mount Wilson Observatory, Angeles National Forest

Timing: Set aside a couple hours to enjoy each observatory. Mount Wilson Observatory is about 33 miles northeast of L.A. via Highway 2/Glendale Freeway and Mount Wilson Red Box Road, about a one-hour drive.

Los Angeles County has two significant observatories for astronomical research. Both are treasured for the cosmic exploration they afford the public, along with panoramic views and scenic surrounding grounds. While one is famed worldwide, the other is less known outside of astronomy circles—but both deserve to be experienced.

Griffith Observatory (2800 E. Observatory Rd., 213/473-0800, http://griffithobservatory.org, free admission), atop Mount Hollywood at an altitude of 1,134 feet in the heart of our urban sprawl, is one of L.A.'s most recognizable icons, featured in films from *Rebel Without a Cause* to *Transformers* to *La La Land*. As a kid, living down the hill from the observatory, I thought it was the highest point in the city, the place closest to the heavens. I imagined that it was a way station for spirits who wandered the empty halls at night, awaiting their turn to ascend to the stars. And that someday I would be one of those spirits.

Opened to the public in 1935, the construction of the observatory in Griffith Park was overseen by leading astronomers and scientists of the day. Then, as now, visitors admired the 40-foot-tall concrete **Astronomers Monument** on the front lawn, the wondrous **Foucault Pendulum** in the central rotunda just past the observatory's ornate front doors, and shows about the cosmos in the **Samuel Oschin Planetarium** (prices vary).

Newer attractions include the **Leonard Nimoy Event Horizon Theater,** with live programs and levels of exhibition space belowground. At **Gunther Depths of Space,** you

the Gunther Depths of Space floor

Foucault Pendulum

dusk at the Griffith Observatory

can get on scales to see what your weight would be on other planets and the Moon, and see *The Big Picture* wall, a massive image of the cosmos—the largest in the world—made especially for the observatory using telescope data. At the **Edge of Space,** the mezzanine overlooking Gunther, learn about meteors and take a photo with a replica of the Moon—as well as see an actual piece of it from the Apollo 14 mission.

But what draws 1.6 million people annually to Griffith Observatory are the priceless panoramic views—especially during our colorful sunsets—from its rooftop promenade and terraces. On a clear day, you can see the Downtown skyline, Santa Monica and the Pacific, and the Mount Wilson Observatory. Use the quarter-operated telescopes for a closer look. But for out-of-this-world views, use the free **public telescopes**—especially the iconic Zeiss refracting telescopes in the rooftop dome. The line at night for viewing can be long, but additional public telescopes are on the observatory lawn and roof, with staff and volunteers happy to direct your eye to celestial points of interest.

L.A. County is also home to the trailblazing but less visited—it gets about 100,000 visitors annually—**Mount Wilson Observatory** (Mt. Wilson Rd., 626/440-9016, www.mtwilson.edu, free admission), founded in 1904 by the astronomer George Ellery Hale and home to the largest telescopes in the world in the early to mid-1900s. Tucked 5,715 feet above sea level in the San Gabriel Mountains northeast of the city, deep in the Angeles National Forest, it offers a wildly different experience than Griffith.

When you arrive at the lower parking lot off Mount Wilson Road, pause to take in the breathtaking views; you'll likely be in the company of others admiring the sea of trees that stretches for miles across the mountains. Then walk the paved fire road that starts just north of the parking lot. The observatory's structures are spread out around the mountain's summit, and this path offers a friendly half-mile walk around the grounds. Signage along the way guides you to the sights. There are no city crowds here, so you can take everything in leisurely; part of the charm of a visit here is wandering from structure to structure in the woods. Or book a two-hour **docent-led walking tour** (Sat.-Sun., $15); it grants special access to some of the attractions.

You'll first come across the small 1936 **Mount Wilson Observatory Museum,** where you can view a miniature model of the grounds and photos captured by the observatory's telescopes. Next, marvel at the 150-foot **Solar Tower;** the telescope within has tracked the sun's activity since 1912. In the structure housing the 100-plus-year-old, 60-foot-tall **Snow Solar Telescope,** weekend volunteers tell you about its history and how it works.

Next up you'll see the dome housing the observatory's **60-inch telescope,** once the world's largest; casual visitors can't enter on their own, but docent-led tours bring you inside so you can look at it. Local lore has it that, after viewing Saturn's rings through this telescope, Griffith J. Griffith (who donated the land for Griffith Park) was disappointed to find out it wasn't open to the public—directly inspiring the creation of Griffith Observatory, where telescopes would be made accessible to everyone to explore the cosmos, free of charge.

From here, walk across the footbridge known as the **"Bridge to the Stars"** (in 1931, Albert Einstein also crossed this bridge) to enter the dome structure housing the observatory's **Hooker 100-inch telescope**—which displaced the 60-inch telescope for a time as the world's largest. Thanks to this telescope, Edwin Hubble and Milton Humason confirmed in

"Bridge to the Stars" leading to the dome housing the 100-inch telescope at Mount Wilson Observatory

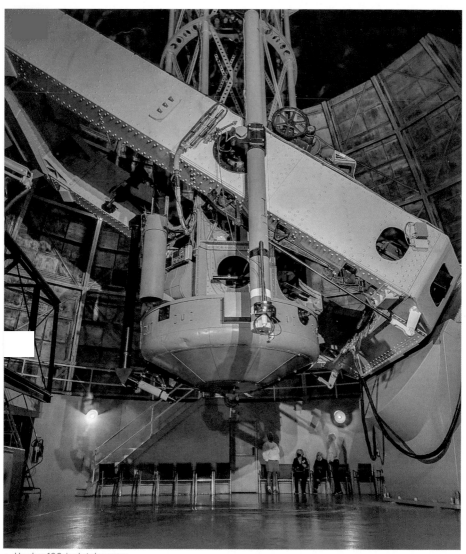

Hooker 100-inch telescope

1929 that the universe was expanding. A stairway leads to a windowed viewing area where you can see the telescope.

To stargaze through the 60-inch and 100-inch telescopes, you'll need to attend **Public Tickets Nights** (60-inch $95, 100-inch $225, ages 12 and over only). Sessions last nearly six hours. The 60- and 100-inch telescopes are also available for group rentals (60-inch $1,050-1,700, 100-inch $2,700-5,000, for up to 25 people); yeah, more than you want to spend—but wow, what a party that would be! Another offering that allows for an intimate experience in the 100-inch telescope dome (though not direct access to the scope) is **Sunday Afternoon Concerts in the Dome** (summer, tickets typically $50), when the space becomes a venue for small jazz or classical ensembles. Mount Wilson Observatory also hosts free **Star Gazing Nights,** where members of the Los Angeles Astronomical Society bring telescopes for the public to use.

Before heading out to Mount Wilson during winter or fire season, check for road closures with **Angeles National Forest** (747/322-6574, www.fs.usda.gov/angeles) or **CalTrans** (800/427-7623, http://roads.dot.ca.gov).

Purchase a $5 Forest Adventure Pass to park at the observatory. You can find it at vendors including Big 5 and REI, but a convenient option on the way is the Shell station in La Cañada Flintridge (4530 Angeles Crest Hwy.). As cell service can be spotty on Mount Wilson, download or print a self-guided tour brochure and map from the observatory's website beforehand.

Connect with . . .
7 Find Griffith Park's hidden gems
23 Bike along the L.A. River

16 Tour Historic Filipinotown by Jeepney

Neighborhoods and City Streets • Art and Culture • For All Ages

Why Go: This Jeepney tour—the only one in the country—offers one of the most thoughtful looks at Filipino American history in L.A.

Where: Tour departure from Pilipino Workers Center (PWC, 153 Glendale Blvd., 213/250-4353, www.pwcsc.org) • Metro bus 10 to Temple St./Glendale Blvd.

Timing: Book a tour at least two weeks in advance. It typically runs 1.5-2 hours.

Filipinos arrived in Los Angeles as early as 1903, and today L.A. has the largest population of Filipino/a/x Americans in the country, numbering nearly half a million—making it the second-largest Filipino metropolitan population after Manila in the Philippines—and there are many FilAm enclaves all over the Southland. As an L.A.-born Filipino American, it's difficult to express what it meant to me when the 2.1-square mile neighborhood near Echo Park received its designation of **Historic Filipinotown** in 2002.

When my dad's family immigrated in the late '60s, they rented a home in Silver Lake, bordering what is now designated Historic Filipinotown—also known as HiFi—and in the years following they, like hundreds of other Filipino families, frequented hangouts in the vicinity. So I was particularly thrilled to take the inaugural **Hidden HiFi Jeepney tour** ($25 adults, $12.50 ages 12 and under and 65 and over, $100 minimum to book), organized by the **Pilipino Workers Center,** when it launched in 2009 and then another, nearly a decade later, this time with my daughter and other kids participating in a summer camp run by the HiFi-based organization Search to Involve Pilipino Americans.

A Jeepney is the predominant form of public transportation in the Philippines. They were constructed from Willys Jeeps left behind by the U.S. military after World War II, and Filipinos often decorate them in glorious fashion, with hood ornaments, horns, and other chrome fixtures, along with eye-catching paint jobs and family names written on the exterior and interior of the vehicles. Jeepneys are open-air vehicles and seat eight adults comfort-

Gintong Kasaysayan, Gintong Pamana mural at Unidad Park by Filipino muralist Eliseo Art Silva

Tribal Cafe

Pilipino Workers Center Jeepney

ably. Riding one around L.A. makes for a thrilling and educational experience. Every time the Jeepney takes to the streets, it brings increased visibility to our community and often-overlooked history. Passing cars and pedestrians will stare—so greet them!

When the tours first launched, they were produced in collaboration with creative studio Public Matters, which developed a mobile media companion for the tour recounting the history of various sites. Your tour can include this accompanying video component, or you can opt for the more low-tech experience: a friendly driver and a knowledgeable and entertaining tour guide who will narrate the area's history from the passenger seat. Just let PWC know your preference.

Departing from PWC's office near Echo Park Lake, the bright orange 1944 Jeepney takes riders by insider businesses only locals would know, along with longtime eateries and public art commemorating FilAm culture and historical figures. At some places you'll pause for a brief stop, while at others you may leave the vehicle to take a closer look. Generally, the tour will also feature two food stops, where guests may purchase items if time allows.

One of the tour sites is **Unidad Park** (1644 Beverly Blvd., www.lanlt.org), home to the magnificent 150-foot-long *Gintong Kasaysayan, Gintong Pamana* ("A Glorious History, A Golden Legacy"), created in 1995 by Filipino muralist Eliseo Art Silva. It's the largest mural depicting Filipino and FilAm history in the United States, featuring notable figures such as farm labor activists Larry Itliong and Philip Vera Cruz and writer Carlos Bulosan. Silva was 22 when his idea was selected from a national pool of proposals; he was driven by the fact that the massive *Great Wall of Los Angeles* mural, whose restoration he worked on as an intern, "did not include a collective story from the Filipino community of Los Angeles." He also designed Historic Filipinotown's **Western Gateway** (Silver Lake Blvd. near W. Temple St.) and **Eastern Gateway** (Beverly Blvd. near Loma Dr.), the latter with architect Celestino Geronimo.

The tour also highlights strip-mall restaurant **Dollar Hits** (2422 W. Temple St., 213/908-6000), known for its Filipino street food and food truck, and **Bahay Kubo** (2330 W. Temple St., 213/413-4804), an eatery my dad's family always goes to, which is called out not only for its *turo turo*-style food—akin to a cafeteria spread where you can enjoy a sampling of dishes—but also for its on-site PNB Remittance Center, where people can send mon-

A Taste of New-School FilAm Culture

You could circle back to some of the legacy eateries covered after the tour for a bite to eat, or patronize some newer-generation FilAm-owned businesses in the area. Feast on Filipino-flavored smoked meat at **The Park's Finest** (1267 W. Temple St., 213/481-2800, www.theparksfinest.com), a casual restaurant opened by Johneric Concordia and Christine Araquel-Concordia in 2012. My family is a big fan of Mama Leah's coconut beef, *timuay* beef tri-tip, and Ann's cornbread *bibingka.* Across the street from Unidad Park, pick up tasty rice bowls with chicken adobo and a veggie take on *sisig*, using eggplant and tofu instead of pork, at takeout spot **Hi-Fi Kitchen** (1667 Beverly Blvd., 213/258-8417, www.hifi-kitchen.com), founded by nurse-turned-chef and HiFi native Justin Foronda in 2018. And enjoy an evening of gin-based cocktails at the oh-so-stylish and dimly lit lounge **Genever** (3123 Beverly Blvd., 213/908-5693, www.geneverla.com), opened in 2018 by my friends, Christine Sumiller, Roselma Samala, and Patricia Perez, to deserving rave reviews.

cy quickly abroad. Where early Filipino hangout Traveler's Cafe used to be, there's now the colorful **Tribal Cafe** (1651 W. Temple St., 213/483-4458, www.tribalcafe.com), owned by FilAm Joshua Jose, offering vegan takes on Filipino dishes and an extensive smoothie menu.

A thoughtful tour stop is the neighborhood **McDonald's** (corner of W. Temple St. and Alvarado St.); this is where FilAm WWII veterans—when they were alive—could be found socializing outside. My *lolo* (grandfather) was a WWII veteran, so hearing the elders called out was a tearjerker moment for me.

The tour concludes with a drive by the **Filipino World War II Veterans Memorial** at **Lake Street Park** (227 N. Lake St., www.laparks.org), installed in 2006 and believed to be the first public art monument honoring Filipino veterans. By artist Cheri Gaulke, the monument is composed of five black granite slabs inscribed with stories and photos she collected by researching the colonial history of the Philippines and meeting with surviving veterans. Two benches face the memorial, and the back of each of the slabs has a letter, together spelling out "Valor."

17 Catch skyline views from Vista Hermosa Natural Park

Get Outside • For All Ages

Why Go: This neighborhood park does double duty, serving up natural wonders and Downtown views that stun.

Where: 100 N. Toluca St. • 323/221-9944 • http://mrca.ca.gov • Metro bus 14 to 1st /Beaudry

Timing: The park is open from dawn to dusk daily. Plan on a couple of hours for an enjoyable visit. Sunset is a popular time to come.

Vista Hermosa Natural Park is an urban treasure perched on a hill hidden from street level. I'd driven past it for years and had no idea it was here, well camouflaged as it is behind tall trees. It took a friend's engagement gathering at the park for me to learn about it. Located between Historic Filipinotown and Downtown, Vista Hermosa is a serene retreat that was designed by landscape architect Mia Lehrer (also responsible for the gardens at the Natural History Museum of Los Angeles County) to bring nature back to an area of the city that lacked green spaces—and it also provides breathtaking views of the skyline we all love. It has a bustling, festive atmosphere on weekends, drawing neighborhood residents and others for picnics and special occasions, as well as for its playground and soccer field.

You can enter the park through the **West Gate** on Toluca Street, where there's a small parking lot, or the **North Gate** on Colton Street. A detailed map of the 10.5-acre park is at both entrances and gives an overview of the easy-to-navigate grounds with well-defined dirt trails and paved walkways.

Near the North Gate entrance is the oval-shaped **Vista Terrace,** an open area bounded by trees and a low wall, one of many places to take in a skyline view at the park. If you stand on the stone-decorated cement wall that doubles as seating, Downtown buildings—including the U.S. Bank Tower, The Ritz-Carlton, and the Bank of America—look as if they're sitting atop the surrounding trees.

view of Downtown from Vista Hermosa Natural Park

▲ Children's Adventure Area

Nearby is the **Children's Adventure Area,** with a large winding snake to walk on and a small slide.

Follow the paths from the playground down to the park's **open green space** or, if you're coming from the West Gate, just follow the stairway or paved pathway up. This area, the center of the multilevel Vista Hermosa, has grassy meadows and picnic-table nooks to find solitude, catch up with friends, or stir romance. Bring a picnic, Frisbee, or croquet set, and maybe even a kite to fly. Or just listen to the sounds of the city (the distant hum of car traffic) and nature (rustling leaves, scurrying squirrels) intermingle. It's also a joy to walk the steep staircases, dirt trails, and winding pathways that cut through the park and let yourself feel engulfed by the plants and trees. Look for signage that points out the flora you might see here, such as California fuchsias, Humboldt lilies, and California sycamores.

Above the central area's **Upper Field** is a modest waterfall and rock grotto that also serves as an **amphitheater,** which hosts nature talks, evening campfires, and kids' programming (call ahead to see what's happening).

view of Downtown from the Lower Field

And you can't leave without taking a picture of yourself at the **Lower Field,** which has a closer view of the Downtown skyline, wonderfully framed by trees. At any hour of the day, you may need to wait your turn to get a solo shot, as many people will be here taking selfies. Or just take a seat and enjoy the view from one of the green benches. This is nature, L.A. style.

Connect with . . .

16 Tour Historic Filipinotown by Jeepney

19 Ride a swan boat (Echo Park Lake)

24 Tour Downtown architecture

18

Go on a bar crawl at Hollywood hotels

Neighborhoods and City Streets • Food and Drink

Why Go: Hollywood's many stylish hotel venues become places to unwind and people-watch come nightfall, when the neighborhood's combination of old-school glamour, colorful party scene, and modern chic really shine.

Where: Multiple locations in Hollywood • Metro B Line (Red) to Hollywood/Vine or Hollywood/Highland

Timing: To truly experience the scene, come on a weekend night and join the crowds.

Attractions along Hollywood Boulevard are world-renowned and visited by thousands each year, so it's no surprise there are many hotels within walking distance. A fun night out among the international crowds can be had hopping between these hotels' bars and eateries for cocktails and bites. In many cities, hotel venues are avoided by the locals and left to the tourists—but in Hollywood, they're often nightlife hot spots, as likely to be frequented by someone who lives around the corner or a celebrity as a traveler.

When night falls, start your crawl at the youngest hotel on this itinerary, the boutique **Kimpton Everly Hotel** (1800 Argyle Ave., 213/279-3532, www.everlyhotelhollywood. com), which opened in 2017. Enter through 1st-floor eatery Jane Q, taking the stairway up to the *Dwell* magazine-worthy hotel lounge. The dimly lit open space is 21st-century chic, with white walls, hardwood floors, modern light fixtures, and a mix of contemporary and midcentury furnishings. It feels more like an L.A. loft living room than a hotel lounge, with a billiards table to boot. Situated in the space is the inviting **Ever Bar** (http://everbarla.com). On the menu there's beer, wine, and themed cocktails—some with cheeky names like Going Back to Cali (a tequila and rosé sour). For more adventurous libations, see if Seth is tending bar and let him take you off-menu: "Give me three ingredients you like, and I'll introduce you to flavors you've never had before," he says. The bar's snack menu includes a charcuterie board, pizzas, and salads. On weekends, crowds come through before or after attending

1: W Hollywood's Living Room **2:** specialty cocktails at Ever Bar **3:** the Tropicana pool **4:** Ever Bar

shows at the nearby Hollywood Pantages Theatre or the Hollywood Bowl. Also in the hotel, on the 5th-floor sundeck, is the highly rated **Yaki Q,** which serves cocktails, yakitori (Japanese-style grilled skewers), and small plates Thursday-Saturday nights with views of the Hollywood skyline, neon signage and all. Reservations are recommended a week in advance.

Next, venture to the **W Hollywood** (6250 Hollywood Blvd., 323/798-1300, www.marriott.com/hotels), a couple of blocks south, and choose the venue that suits your liking. The hotel's decor is on brand, with bright, poppy colors, artwork, and loud patterned carpeting, but gets taken up a Hollywood notch—case in point, the massive chandelier in the **Living Room** lounge area—beneath which DJs spin on the weekend and the lights are turned down low. Off the lounge is the entrance for the **Delphine Eatery & Bar** (www.delphinehollywood.com), good for reliable contemporary American fare (people love the oysters). Specialty cocktails, appetizers, and dinner are also available at the outdoor **Station Hollywood** bar, which has plenty of comfortable seating and two fire pits going on each side for dramatic effect.

Finally, step back into Hollywood's past, ending your evening at **The Hollywood Roosevelt** (7000 Hollywood Blvd., 323/856-1970, www.thehollywoodroosevelt.com), which opened in 1927. It embodies Hollywood glamour at its best. Walk west from the W on the boulevard for a mile and take in the **Hollywood Walk of Fame** (http://walkoffame.com) en route to mingle with the tourists if you like, or avoid the commotion at street level and jump on the Metro at Hollywood and Vine for a six-minute ride to the Hollywood and Highland station. Here, too, you can take your pick of places. Enter the Roosevelt's lobby lounge through one of its many archways and enjoy the decorative vaulted ceilings, indoor palm trees, small fountain, and cushioned seating areas. A **lobby bar** is at the far end and, in addition to drinks, serves small plates from The Barish steakhouse, by James Beard Award-winning chef Nancy Silverton. The mood here is low-key, with a fireplace and warm lighting that lends itself to intimate conversations. For a more animated setting, venture to the 1960s-era pool area to grab a drink at the **Tropicana Bar and Café,** where you'll be surrounded by towering palm trees against the night sky. It's so Old Hollywood in its glitz that it always makes me smile. The Tropicana transforms into a party scene during special events, when guests are encouraged to dress according to theme. Maybe you'll experience

The Hollywood Roosevelt's lobby

an '80s night with food and drink in tune with that decade or one of the Tuesday Tropicana Movie Nights. Check the calendar for what's coming up (admission fee and advance tickets required). Also in the hotel is **The Spare Room,** featuring board games and two bowling lanes to go along with $18 cocktails. With such spirited names as the Cha-Ching, Tannic at the Disco, and Cashmere Dagger, does it matter what's in them? For some food to top off your night out, you'll find diner fare at the hotel's **25 Degrees.**

Connect with . . .

3 Feast on famous chicken in Hollywood

8 Sample late-night tacos on Sunset Boulevard

19 Ride a swan boat

Get Outside • For All Ages

Why Go: Enjoy distinct pedal boat experiences at two lakes—a pastoral respite at one and an urban delight at the other.

Where: Echo Park Lake and Lake Balboa • Metro bus 92 to Glendale/Santa Ynez or LADOT Pico Union/Echo Park DASH bus to Echo Park Ave./Laguna Ave. (Echo Park Lake), Metro G Line (Orange) bus to Balboa Station or Metro bus 164 to Victory/Petit (Lake Balboa)

Timing: Pedal boat rides at these parks are available year-round during the day, weather permitting. Night rides are also offered at Echo Park Lake.

Two parks in the vicinity of the city have artificial lakes with swan pedal boats just begging to be enjoyed. Based on my unscientific survey (conversations with extended family and circle of friends), few locals have. And while the themed watercraft—managed by the same SoCal company—may be the same, the experience at each lake is otherwise wildly different. Either makes for a fun destination on its own, or you might challenge yourself—as I did—to do them both in a day to enjoy the contrast (note, though, that freeway traffic on the 101 means the drive between the lakes can take as little as 30 minutes—or more than an hour).

A trip to the San Fernando Valley's 27-acre **Lake Balboa** in **Anthony C. Beilenson Park** (6300 Balboa Blvd., Van Nuys, 818/437-7559, http://wheelfunrentals.com, hourly rates $11 adults, $6 children) makes for a good afternoon activity. Bring a picnic to enjoy on the grass or at one of the covered picnic areas, or patronize one of the food vendors around the park. Then head to the southeastern edge of the lake, where the cheery swan boats are docked. The pedal boats come with two or five seats, and thankfully have shade canopies to protect you from the sun. Attendants will get you suited up in a required life jacket and give you basic steering instructions. When I asked how many phones they've seen perish in the lake, one said, "Many" (take note). What you'll immediately notice while pedaling around Lake Balboa is what's absent from your view: buildings of any kind, except the few park

Lake Balboa swan boat

swan boats and lotus beds on Echo Park Lake at magic hour

swan boats on Echo Park Lake at night

structures. This is what makes the lake such a great nearby getaway. What you will see are lush surroundings, distant mountains, and families of geese and ducks (and, if you're lucky, ducklings just learning to swim!). There's even a beautiful, if humble, waterfall at one end of the lake. If you visit in spring, you'll also get to see the park's 500 or so Japanese cherry blossom trees in bloom, making for an even more picturesque ride. When you're done, cool down with an icy treat; I recommend a mango *paleta* (a Mexican popsicle) with *chamoy* (pickled fruit) or chile from one of the mobile carts or the ice cream truck in the parking lot.

Echo Park Lake (751 Echo Park Ave., 213/444-9445, http://wheelfunrentals.com, hourly rates $11 adults, $6 children) is best experienced at sunset. Be forewarned that finding parking close by is the biggest challenge of a visit here. Give yourself some time to walk around the park if you haven't visited before. During summer, beautiful lotus beds blanket the edges of the 29-acre lake. A constant attraction are the lake's geese and duck residents. Make sure to keep track of time, because you'll want to be on the water to catch sunset. Head to the boathouse, near the middle of the lake on the east side, then board your swan, here

Echo Park's Lotus Festival

Timed to when lotus flowers are in bloom on Echo Lake—which reportedly has the largest lotus bed in the country—Echo Park plays host to the city's annual two-day **Lotus Festival** (www.laparksfoundation.org, summer, free). The event, a celebration of Asian Pacific cultures, was first held in 1972. The neighborhood was selected because of its central location near many Asian neighborhoods: Little Bangladesh, Historic Filipinotown, Little Tokyo, Chinatown, and Koreatown. Each year a different country and its traditions and food are prominently highlighted, along with other Asian or Pacific Islander artists, artisans, and eateries. Visitors can enjoy a series of live performances in the park, ranging from local dance and musical groups to martial arts demonstrations and spoken word performances. One of the main attractions is the dragon boat races, which draw fans every year.

equipped with LED lights. (To see the colorful, now-retired Echo Park pedal boats of my youth, watch the Beastie Boys' 1992 "Netty's Girl" music video, directed by Tamra Davis). Steer into the open water, careful to avoid the many boats filled with visitors, who are all here for the same reason you are: views from the lake of the Downtown skyline at golden hour, made more magical by the lake's three-geyser fountain shooting high into the sky, providing a light shower as you pass by. As the sun goes down and the city lights start to flicker on, take your feet off the pedals and linger, if you thought the views were impressive during the day, at night, they're a dream. With all the swan boats alight on the lake, you'll experience a very "I love L.A." moment.

Neighborhoods and City Streets • Art and Culture • Food and Drink • Shopping

Why Go: In the space of a few blocks, you'll find a hub for BIPOC and women entrepreneurs, creators, artisans, and chefs.

Where: On W. Adams Blvd., between S. Burnside Ave. and S. Cochran Ave. • Metro bus 37 to Adams/Dunsmuir

Timing: Give yourself an afternoon to shop, drink, eat, and especially chat with people in the neighborhood—they're what will make you want to return again and again.

The West Adams area of South Los Angeles has long been prized for its notable architecture—it's one of the oldest neighborhoods in the city, with many designated Historic-Cultural Monuments. In recent years, the diverse neighborhood has drawn outside attention for its burgeoning businesses—many female- and BIPOC-owned—concentrated along a stretch of **West Adams Boulevard** that beats with creative energy day and night.

A major destination on this stretch is contemporary gallery **Band of Vices** (5351 W. Adams Blvd., 323/481-6878, www.bandofvices.com), showcasing works by artists from predominantly marginalized communities. It started in a modest space nearby in 2015 and since then has secured a two-room, 4,800-square-foot space that can't be missed—both literally and figuratively: Its exterior is painted a shade of hot pink called Beauty Queen, specifically chosen by founder and West Adams resident Terrell Tilford as "a love letter to artists and to the community to say that we deserve something really beautiful that we can engage with." While the rapid development of the area (and the gentrification it brings) is of concern to residents, Tilford, a native of South L.A., hopes his gallery inspires future generations. He specifically mentioned a five-year-old resident in the neighborhood who visits often: "Who knows? He might become an artist . . . and tell the story how some guy 'told me I could be a rock star, and here I am.'" At the expanded space's 2021 opening show, *C11H17NO3 (Mescaline)*, vibrant and energetic large-scale works—sculptures, mixed media, paintings—

Ruben Morancy, the late sommelier and cofounder of Adams Wine Shop

handcrafted goods at The Global Trunk showroom

Band of Vices founder Terrell Tilford with paintings by (left) Ariel Vargassal, *Cockfight*, 2018, and (right) Patrick Henry Johnson, *Black Girl Magic: Shani Hula Hooping on the Beach While Changing the Cosmos to Shrooms!*, 2021

questioned what our future holds as we come out of a pandemic that isolated us from one another. I was most taken by acclaimed L.A. artist Patrick Henry Johnson's *Black Girl Magic,* a painting of a sunglasses- and bikini-wearing woman, local "hoopologist" Shani Anne Marvelous, joyously hula-hooping on a beach against an orange and pink sky, with colorful mushrooms floating about her.

Directly next door to Band of Vices is **Adams Wine Shop** (5357 W. Adams Blvd., 323/420-6750, http://adamswineshop.com), with a neon sign and bright red awning. What the woman behind the counter shared with me on my visit immediately had my attention: "We specialize in wines by either women winemakers or people of color." She introduced me to the sommelier and shop cofounder, Ruben Morancy, who enthusiastically discussed their inventory. Most bottles in the 150-plus collection run in the reasonably priced range of $15-30, and the shop offers 14 wines by the glass as well as wine tastings in its narrow but airy space. Choose a flight of three or opt for Flights and Bites—with bites provided by the neighboring modern Cali-soul food eatery **Alta Adams** (5359 W. Adams Blvd., 323/571-4999, http://altaadams.com), under the same management as the wine shop and run by chef and Watts native Keith Corbin with chef Daniel Patterson. Along with wine tastings, the flight includes your choice of one of three small Alta dishes (a piece of fried chicken or black-eyed peas, for instance). If you're hungry for more, try Corbin's gravy-topped oxtails and rice (if you can snag an order—it often sells out). I left Adams Wine Shop with a bottle of Aslina 2020 Sauvignon Blanc, at Morancy's recommendation; it's by the first South African female winemaker, Ntsiki Biyela. Morancy has sadly since passed away, but the shop continues his vision.

A block east is **Antiqua** (5335 W. Adams Blvd. #106, 310/384-3178, http://antiquajewelry.com), owned by Iris Yona, who has been in business for more than 25 years. She makes the majority of the jewelry on display by hand, and her collection consists primarily of delicate pieces featuring an array of gems and precious stones. Also here are gift items, many of which are also produced by local artisans, such as ceramics, plants, candles, bags, tunics, and a small selection of books and accessories for the whole family, including scarves and socks.

Across the street is the small showroom for **The Global Trunk** (5370 W. Adams Blvd., 323/433-7170, http://theglobaltrunk.com), owned by Josetta Sbeglia and Cathy Benavides, who work to create sustainable opportunities for artisans in Guatemala and Mexico. Their colorful collection of handmade and embroidered pillows, blankets, bags, and children's clothing are made in collaboration with the artisans. Some pieces reflect the personal style of the artisan or preserve traditional cultural designs or weaving practices, while the brand introduces more modern flourishes to other items.

Two storefronts west is the original location of Band of Vices, renamed **coLAB** (5376 W. Adams Blvd.), where other creatives and curators now showcase work. The space might host a public event or an exhibit—such as one I saw, a collection of paintings by artists of color curated by Bronx-based Kiara Cristina Ventura—or serve as an incubator meeting place. And you never know who you might meet here. Talking with Joshua, a friendly attendant at coLAB, about how much I loved the *C11H17NO3 (Mescaline)* show and my favorite piece there, he smiled and said, "That's my dad."

Connect with . . .

33 Dance while you browse at Crenshaw Mall's Saturday markets
34 Delve into the world's largest LGBTQ collection at ONE Archives

21 Celebrate life and death during Día de los Muertos

Entertainment and Events • Art and Culture • For All Ages

Why Go: Join thousands of Angelenos across L.A. for events that honor the lives and legacies of the deceased.

Where: Citywide

Timing: Día de los Muertos (Day of the Dead) is observed on November 1 and 2, but many local organizations and public sites have altars on display and events starting in October.

The city comes alive in celebratory and colorful fashion to remember the lives of lost loved ones during **Día de los Muertos** (called "Día de Muertos" in Mexico), or Day of the Dead, an ancient holiday traced back to the Aztecs, who resided in what is present-day central and southern Mexico. Incorporating Indigenous and Catholic Church traditions, it embraces death as part of the cycle of life—not the end of it. Today, Día de los Muertos is observed throughout Latin America, the Caribbean, and U.S. cities like Los Angeles that have a large Mexican American population. During the holiday, it's thought that the souls of the dead can return to the world of the living to be with their loved ones. Families visit and decorate loved ones' graves and, at home, create altars (*ofrendas*) for them, including items such as photos, personal mementos, and candles, as well as food, drink, and flowers—particularly marigolds—to welcome them back. Public celebrations often include community altars, processions, dancing, and singing.

The site of a long-running Día de los Muertos festival is at Downtown's **El Pueblo de Los Angeles Historical Monument** (125 Paseo de la Plaza, 213/485-6855, http://elpueblo.lacity.org), the city's oldest district, with buildings dating to the 1800s. The merchants of the brick-lined **Olvera Street** (http://discoverolverastreet.com), a Mexican marketplace founded in 1930 just off the plaza, organize a mostly free, nine-day event (Oct. 25-Nov. 2, www.olveraevents.com), with most activities—including live music and dance performanc-

La Calavera Catrina at Hollywood Forever Cemetery

altar on display at Grand Park

Ballet Folklorico Mexico Azteca dancers preparing to perform at El Pueblo's bandstand

es—taking place around El Pueblo's plaza and *kiosko* (bandstand). The **Novenario Procession** kicks off the festival and includes a Mayan blessing and an Aztec group that leads people through the plaza, as well as a performance by Aztec dancers. Public altars are on display, and a nightly theater show produced by **Teatro del Barrio** traces the Indigenous roots of the sacred holiday.

About a 15-minute walk west from El Pueblo is the gift to the city that is **Grand Park** (200 N. Grand Ave., 213/972-8080, http://grandparkla.org), with its large open lawns, native plant gardens, performance stages, and the city's favorite splash pad, among other attractions. This is where thousands of Angelenos gather to celebrate L.A.'s biggest public parties of the year, including New Year's Eve and July 4th celebrations. It also hosts free Día de los Muertos events and large-scale *ofrendas* (late Oct.-early Nov.) by artists and community organizations in collaboration with Self-Help Graphics & Art. Past programming has included the traditional **Noche de Ofrenda (Night of the Offerings)** ceremony, featuring an Indigenous community-led blessing and communal circle as well as Aztec art-inspired workshops.

Self-Help Graphics & Art (1300 E. 1st St., 323/881-6444, www.selfhelpgraphics. com/diadelosmuertos), founded in 1970 to provide Chicano/a and Latinx artists a community space, also hosts many free Día de los Muertos-themed events from its base in Boyle Heights, attracting more than 10,000 people each year. In fact, Self-Help Graphics played a pivotal role in popularizing the holiday in the city; its first **Annual Día de los Muertos Exhibition and Celebration** was held in 1972—making it the longest-running public event celebrating the holiday in the country. Festivities kick off Saturdays in October with a series of workshops in traditional crafts, such as marigold paper flowers and papier-mâché. Other unique events have included two "wheeled" processions to honor ancestors: a bike ride, **Bike Ofrenda,** during which you may find yourself riding alongside cyclists dressed as skeletons, and a **Día de los Muertos Car Caravan,** a drive from East L.A. to Boyle Heights. Participants are encouraged to decorate their modes of transport in the spirit of the season. The main event, held on or near November 2, features a blessing and procession, live performances, arts and crafts, and food vendors.

Join thousands of festively attired people at the **Hollywood Forever Cemetery**

(6000 Santa Monica Blvd., 323/469-1181, www.ladayofthedead.com), generally on the Saturday before or on November 2. The East Hollywood cemetery's event is said to be the largest of its kind outside of Mexico. Daytime ($40) and nighttime ($50) tickets are required for general admission. On the cemetery's spacious grounds, more than 100 altars are on display, and existing graves are decorated in magnificent fashion. There are also traditional and folkloric dances, art exhibits, and culinary vendors. An endless parade of thematically and stunningly dressed and made-up attendees draw your attention at every turn.

Plaza de la Raza Cultural Center for the Arts & Education (3540 N. Mission Rd., 323/223-2475, www.plazadelaraza.org), which provides multidisciplinary, intergenerational arts education to the city's Eastside neighborhoods, holds free Día de los Muertos festivities at its lakeside location in Lincoln Park. Its event takes place on the evening of November 1. Community altars are displayed on its plaza, with one central altar where visitors are welcome to add artifacts and photos of lost loved ones. Mariachi bands (sometimes all-female groups!), dancers, and many of the organization's student ensemble groups perform on an outdoor stage. In the neighboring **Plaza Boathouse Gallery,** built in 1912, you can view themed artwork by local artists and browse goods by artisan vendors. There are also arts-and-crafts workshops that may include activities such as making *calaveras* (sugar skulls), piñatas, or masks. "The point is to remember our loved ones, that is how we keep them alive. Forgetting is the final death, so celebrate the life," says Tomas Benitez of Plaza de la Raza. "Death is not to be feared, it is to be embraced as part of life. And we celebrate as a family and community. And we welcome any and all to join us; we share our culture with America."

Connect with . . .

❷ See all-female mariachi bands
❸⓪ Find unexpected art and culture in L.A.'s cemeteries
❸⑥ Get creative with local artisans

22 Eat with your hands in Little Ethiopia

Food and Drink • Neighborhoods and City Streets

Why Go: Dine along a vibrant one-block stretch of Fairfax offering authentic Ethiopian cuisine.

Where: S. Fairfax Ave. between Olympic Blvd. and Whitworth Dr. • Metro bus 217 to Fairfax/Olympic or Fairfax/Whitworth

Timing: Enjoy a long meal into the evening to experience the avenue as it quiets down (once rush hour has passed) and see the neighborhood's neon signage light up.

The constant flow of cars through the narrow two-lane stretch of Fairfax in **Little Ethiopia** does little to disrupt the unrushed mood here; this neighborhood has always felt to me like it moves to its own rhythms. Maybe it's the hours I tend to visit it, just before dusk, when L.A. is at its prettiest and the neighborhood's neon signs and colorful storefronts really captivate. Or maybe it's the comforting sense of community you feel as soon as you step onto the sidewalk here.

I had driven through Little Ethiopia for years without stopping until my then-university classmates made the strip our go-to for dinner gatherings. The family-owned restaurants here offer consistently friendly service, affordable communal dining (a necessity on our student budgets), and a fun, utensil-free dining experience. We loved sitting around the traditional platter featuring a large piece of *injera,* tearing off bits to use for scooping up the flavorful dishes served on it. Add in the typically low-lit ambience amid lushly draped and ornately designed eating nooks, and these meals in Little Ethiopia succeeded in completely transporting us out of our hectic lives—and still do.

For a first visit to the neighborhood, I suggest walking from one end of the Fairfax block between Olympic and Whitworth—the busiest stretch of Little Ethiopia—to the other, checking out each storefront to see what beckons.

Or you might do as I recently did with my visiting friend and former Angeleno Anna,

▲ Rosalind's Restaurant combo platter

who had never been to Little Ethiopia: Head to the restaurant that kick-started it all. The first seed of this tight-knit enclave was planted by immigrant Fekere Gebre-Mariam, who in 1989 opened **Rosalind's Restaurant** (1044 S. Fairfax Ave., 323/936-2486, www.rosalindsla. com), the first Ethiopian eatery on the block. Today at Rosalind's, various sit-down areas entice, including an intimate wood-enclosed corner booth, tables with their own wood-sculptured roofs overhead, and a traditional big-party area with a banquette, leather stools, and *messobs* in the middle. But it was too nice of a night to stay in for our meal, so we took an outdoor table next to one of the neon signs before ordering one of my favorite appetizers, a beef *sambusa* (a pastry spiced with herbs and jalapeños), continuing on to a selection of meat dishes (chicken, lamb, beef) and items like *gomen* (collard greens), *shiro* (spiced chickpeas), *kek* (yellow split peas), and *fassolia* (string beans and carrots), all served on a single platter.

Directly across the street from Rosalind's is **Messob Ethiopian Restaurant** (1041 S. Fairfax Ave., 323/938-8827, www.messob.com); at Gebre-Mariam's urging, then-owner Rahel Woldmedhin brought her restaurant to the district two years after Rosalind's opened (cur-

▲ Little Ethiopia's Fairfax Avenue

rently owned by brothers Berhanu and Getahun Asfaw, Messob is named for the traditional Ethiopian breadbasket that doubles as a serving table). The two restaurants anchored the burgeoning community. In the decade that followed, during which a wave of Ethiopian immigrants arrived in Los Angeles, more Ethiopian entrepreneurs and residents followed them to the area, also called "Little Addis" after the country's capital city. By 2002, the stretch of Fairfax between Olympic and Pico was officially deemed Little Ethiopia, thanks to the business owners, community organizations, and residents who campaigned for the designation.

After dinner, browse **Merkato Ethiopian Restaurant and Market** (1036 1/2 S. Fairfax Ave., 323/935-1775, http://merkatorestaurant.com), whose bright signage has the colorful Ethiopian flag as its background. It has a large selection of spices and jewelry as well as incense and scented oils. Two storefronts down, you can shop more shelves of spices plus Ethiopian coffee at **Buna Ethiopian Food and Market** (1034 S. Fairfax Ave., 323/964-9731, http://bunaethiopianmarket.com), or enjoy freshly prepared dishes in the small eatery.

I highly recommend ending your evening with dessert at **Rahel Vegan Cuisine** (1047 S. Fairfax Ave., 323/937-8401, http://rahelvegancuisine.com), open since 2005 and named for chef Woldmedhin—who left Messob to open this 100 percent vegan restaurant. We opted for tasty, calming ginger tea and cheesecake, but other yummy options include a baklava and vegan mango cake.

Connect with . . .

⓫ Watch movies in historic theaters (New Beverly Cinema)
⓴ Shop for art and wine in West Adams

23 Bike along the L.A. River

Iconic L.A. • Get Outside • Neighborhoods and City Streets

Why Go: The L.A. River is one of the wonders of the city, yet many residents have never explored its banks. A stretch of the river from Griffith Park to Elysian Valley is particularly magical.

Where: L.A. River Bike Path, starting at Griffith Park • http://lariver.org, http://lariverrecreation.org

Timing: A casual bike ride along the river on this suggested 3.6-mile (one-way) route takes about 20-30 minutes, but you'll want to give yourself hours to enjoy.

Bike- and pedestrian-friendly paved paths line the 51-mile L.A. River, which cuts through Central Los Angeles. I used to watch in amazement and envy from the car window while sitting in rush-hour traffic on the 5 as cyclists along the sometimes-parallel path sped by. So I joined them, and there's nothing like experiencing this river trail on a set of two wheels. While you could walk it, you'll cover more of the river faster and enjoy the feeling of the wind blowing through your hair on a bike. This ride from Griffith Park to Elysian Valley includes a variety of parks and neighborhood eateries along the way. But the star attraction of the ride is the river itself: Thanks to being one of three sections of the L.A. River that has a soft bottom (no concrete), this stretch—known as the **Glendale Narrows**—flows with biodiversity; you may spot snowy egrets, sandpipers, herons, and woodpeckers.

A great place to start a ride along the river is the **Crystal Springs Picnic Area,** located just east of the **Griffith Park Ranger Center and Visitor's Center** (4730 Crystal Springs Dr., 323/644-2050), which has a small lobby and nature exhibit highlighting wildlife and plants native to the park. If you don't have your own wheels, **Spokes 'N Stuff** (323/662-6573, www.spokes-n-stuff.com, Memorial Day-Labor Day) offers bike rentals and is conveniently located right next to the ranger station. From here, you'll need to walk your bike (riding isn't allowed on the trail or tunnel prior to) for about 10 minutes to the river path. Head east to the **Main Trail,** on which you'll turn right to head south; the trail runs

1: Spoke Bicycle Cafe 2: love lock bridge at Sunnynook River Park 3: skipping stones on the L.A. River 4: locals taking in the view

adjacent to the freeway until you reach the tunnel that leads to the **L.A. River Bike Path.** You'll emerge right at the entry of the car-free **La Kretz Bridge,** or North Atwater Bridge, where you can hop on your bike. Designed for pedestrian, bicycle, and equestrian traffic and featuring a massive white mast that's more than 100 feet high, with cables radiating from it, it's a sight to see, drawing both ire and praise from neighbors.

From here you'll venture south on the bike path and see many parks along the river—each worth visiting. Travel just over a mile to the small but quaint **Sunnynook River Park,** with a pedestrian bridge over the river that locals have transformed into L.A.'s own love lock bridge.

If you're ready for a treat, cross the river just south of the park via the **Red Car Bridge,** which will put you on Atwater Village's main drag, Glendale Boulevard, populated with a variety of eateries and independently owned boutiques. Cool down with artisanal ice cream at **Wanderlust Creamery** (3134 Glendale Blvd., 818/774-9888, www.wanderlustcreamery. com). Try such Filipino-inspired flavors as Pandan Tres Leches or Ube Malted Crunch.

Back on the path, head a mile south from Sunnynook. Right after you pass under the 1927 **Fletcher Drive Bridge,** a Historic-Cultural Monument, you'll reach the small **Rattlesnake Park.** Snap a photo in front of artist and river activist Brett Goldstone's *Great Heron Gates.* A half mile farther along the tree-lined trail is Elysian Valley's picturesque **Lewis MacAdams Riverfront Park,** with grassy areas and picnic tables, plus a large dirt bowl visitors can bike and a snake sculpture to climb.

For a close-by option for sustenance, continue about a half mile down the bike path from Lewis MacAdams Riverfront Park to **Spoke Bicycle Cafe** (3050 N. Coolidge Ave., 323/684-1130, www.spokebicyclecafe.com) to enjoy quality fare and drinks on a spacious patio. You can also get a tune-up at the café's bike repair shop (which also has rentals).

Or, for a great hearty meal or happy-hour option (even with kids in tow) on your way back to Griffith Park, take the **Baum Bicycle Bridge** (between the Red Car Bridge and La Kretz Bridge) to cross the river at Los Feliz Boulevard and make your way to Scottish pub **Morrison** (3179 Los Feliz Blvd., 323/667-1839, www.morrisonrestaurant.com), which is gloriously decorated for holidays throughout the year. Your order sometimes comes with a vinyl balloon, whatever your age (just ask).

Other Ways to Enjoy the L.A. River

For a deeper dive into the river's many offerings, **Friends of the Los Angeles River** (FoLAR, 323/223-0585, http://folar.org), founded by L.A. writer Lewis MacAdams, offers downloadable maps (look under the "Get Involved" section) and private river tours. Contribute to keeping the L.A. River clean and make new friends by participating in one of FoLAR's year-round cleanups. If you feel like kayaking, book a ride in the area with **L.A. River Expeditions** (818/221-5218, www.lariverexpeditions.org, Memorial Day-Labor Day) or **L.A. River Kayak Safari** (747/272 7317, http://lariverkayaksafari.org, May 30-Sept. 30).

Along your ride, you'll encounter Angelenos of all kinds: the aggressive bikers, dressed in full racing gear, who quickly pass, calling out "On your left!" and the cruising bikers and skaters who blare their music so loud on their speakers that their river soundtrack becomes yours. You'll also see folks sweating away doing reps at outdoor fitness zones along the way. The L.A. River isn't pristine—along some parts, you'll see piles of trash and debris strewn about. But it's very much a part of the city, showcasing L.A. nature and grit all in one.

Connect with . . .

7 Find Griffith Park's hidden gems

15 See stars at L.A. County's observatories

24 Tour Downtown architecture

Iconic L.A. • Art and Culture • Neighborhoods and City Streets

Why Go: Informative walking tours led by the Los Angeles Conservancy will deepen your appreciation for the cityscape.

Where: Tour departure from Pershing Square (bounded by S. Hill and S. Olive St. and W. 5th and W. 6th St.) • Metro B Line (Red) to Pershing Square

Timing: The L.A. Conservancy's Historic Downtown Walking Tour usually takes place Saturday mornings and lasts 2.5 hours. Tours sell out, so reserve at least two weeks in advance; September, October, and December tend to be less busy.

Since 1980, the **Los Angeles Conservancy** (532 W. 6th St., Ste. 82, 213/623-2489, www.laconservancy.org) has offered public walking tours of the city's architectural gems. Tour fees support the organization, which advocates for the preservation of uniquely L.A. sites. The threat of demolition of the can't-imagine-the-city-without-it Los Angeles Central Library, built in 1926, prompted the nonprofit's formation in 1978.

The organization's various offerings span explorations of Downtown's art deco architecture, modern skyline, historic movie palaces, iconic Union Station, and more, but its most popular offering is its **Historic Downtown Walking Tour** ($15 general public, $10 conservancy members and ages 17 and under). It covers about 14 sites (some exteriors and some interiors) over the course of 12 blocks, with stairs and hills.

On the day I took the tour our docent was Dylan, who enthusiastically imparted details about L.A.'s history while lending insight into how the city's built environment came to be. I found it endearing that even well into the 21st century, Dylan carried a binder of archival images to share, just as the docent had on the first L.A. Conservancy tour I took in 1999. (The passionate docents and memorable Angelenos and out-of-town visitors you'll meet in your group, which is typically capped at 12 people, are as much a part of the experience of the tour as the architecture.) The Historic Downtown tour can spur your love for (or feed your frustration with) our city's mix of architectural styles, as you learn about design trends and the ways

1: Angels Flight **2:** quintessential L.A. mix of architectural styles **3:** docent Dylan **4:** Grand Central Market

key individuals, city budgets, and events influenced them. Why did the architects of the **L.A. Central Library** (630 W. 5th St.) top it with a pyramid versus a dome? Why do the post-1960s office buildings of **Bunker Hill** have such spacious open plazas? And how were the architects of the art deco-style **Title Guarantee & Trust Building** (411 W. 5th St.), constructed in 1930, able to bypass the city's height limits? Such questions will be answered on this tour.

Among the highlights are riding the 1901 two-car funicular **Angels Flight** (351 S. Hill St., www.angelsflight.org, $1 one-way), which takes passengers between Hill Street and Grand Avenue, and seeing inside the 1893 Romanesque Revival-style **Bradbury Building** (304 S. Broadway), whose stunning Victorian court has appeared in movies including *Double Indemnity, Blade Runner,* and *(500) Days of Summer.*

As we strolled by examples of Beaux Arts and Moderne architecture, as well as late 20th-century towering skyscrapers, I was reminded of how quickly change at the street level happens in our city. I was stunned to see the elimination of the spectacular water features at Bunker Hill's **California Plaza** (300 S. Grand Ave.); apparently they were quite costly

▲ Bradbury Building

to maintain. And as we walked through the **Grand Central Market** (317. S. Market), open since 1917, my family was surprised to find that the fresh produce and dried foods stands have largely been replaced by artisan wares and trendy eateries, with just a couple of legacy tenants remaining. Thankfully, the docents call out such history so that it's not forgotten.

Docents also share facts that Angelenos will not be proud of—the displacement and segregation of communities of color due to racist housing covenants, redlining, and other discriminatory practices that still exist today. They also take the time to acknowledge the Gabrielino/Tongva, the original caretakers of the land that is now the L.A. Basin, showing what their dwellings looked like and how they were constructed. "We have been striving to make sure that our tours don't just showcase breathtaking architecture, but also include stories and sites that represent the histories of all the people who live in Los Angeles," said program manager Alex Inshishian. "Historic preservation isn't just about unique architecture, or famous architects."

I was particularly moved that the tour ended at **Biddy Mason Memorial Park** (333 S. Spring St.), where the prominent L.A. entrepreneur and philanthropist's home once stood. Today, the pocket park features an 80-foot-long concrete wall by artist Sheila Levrant de Bretteville (whom I had coincidentally interviewed just months earlier) that features a timeline of Biddy's remarkable life, from being born enslaved to owning land in Los Angeles—among the first African American women to do so—and cofounding the First African Methodist Episcopal Church in 1872.

To prepare for your tour, bring a water bottle and a good camera, and wear comfortable walking shoes. Then let all of your senses be stimulated. Soak up the sounds of the streets and traffic. Take in the aromas of food wafting out of restaurants. Touch the ironwork and sculpted banisters in century-old buildings. Be transported to the city's yesteryears as you walk our gum-spotted sidewalks.

Connect with . . .

🔞 Buy fresh blooms in the Flower District

🔢 Catch skyline views from Vista Hermosa Natural Park

🔢 Steep yourself in the city's teahouse culture (Rendezvous Court)

25 Go on a lakeside walk beneath the Hollywood Sign

Get Outside • For All Ages

Why Go: See the iconic sign from a local perspective on a walk around the scenic Hollywood Reservoir.

Where: Hollywood Reservoir in the Hollywood Hills

Timing: Allow yourself at least an hour to walk this 3.3-mile loop.

Located deep in the Hollywood Hills between the 101 to the west and Griffith Park to the east, the **Hollywood Reservoir**—also known as **Lake Hollywood**—and the Mulholland Dam that forms it are hidden treasures that even many Angelenos don't know about. Constructed in the middle of a hilly populated neighborhood, it was considered an engineering marvel when it was completed in 1924. You could see the face of the dam from miles away until the early 1930s, when earth was added to shore up the dam's wall and vegetation was planted to camouflage it on the hillside. Now you can't see it from the streets below, helping keep this spot something of a locals' secret; its secluded location means it's primarily free of crowds.

A paved road circumnavigates the upper and lower reservoir and grants stunning views on an easy walk. There are a couple of main access points. On the northern end of the reservoir is the **North Gate** (Lake Hollywood Dr., off Wonder View Dr.) and on the southern end is the **Hollywood Reservoir Trailhead** (at the terminus of Weidlake Dr.). Ample street parking is available along Lake Hollywood Drive at the North Gate, and the Hollywood Reservoir Trailhead has a small parking lot. Portable bathrooms and water stations are at each trailhead.

I enjoy starting at the Hollywood Reservoir Trailhead to frontload the most awe-inspiring views. This entrance will put you directly at the concrete **Mulholland Dam** and reservoir; walk over the dam and enjoy unobstructed views of the body of water below and the **Hollywood Sign** on Mount Lee above in the distance. Having seen the sign from more

△ view of the Hollywood Sign from the Mulholland Dam

△ Mulholland Dam

⌃ biking across the Mulholland Dam

⌃ a view of the upper reservoir

common and congested vantages like Griffith Park makes seeing it on a hillside above the serene reservoir and its natural landscaping that much more awesome. The dam is also a beauty, with wonderfully sculpted archways—look closely and you'll notice the protruding heads of bears between each, a nod to California's wildlife—and was named after chief engineer William Mulholland. As the designer of L.A.'s early aqueducts and reservoirs, his name graces many of the city's structures (along with a famous street). This reservoir used to be a water source for residents but now is for emergency use only.

Once you cross the dam, you'll continue in a clockwise loop around the reservoir, with different vantages of the Hollywood Sign along the way. If you're here on a clear day, the views go on for miles, but an overcast day offers equally memorable views of the clouds reflected in the reservoir. Admire the water to one side of you and a sea of greenery, including pine and eucalyptus, to the other. You might catch sight of mule deer or desert cottontail, or encounter snakes; we saw a baby one slithering near the fence line around the reservoir. Bask in the quiet of the hills, just miles from the busy Hollywood Walk of Fame.

The path is used by walkers, casual bike riders, and excited little kids on scooters. Dogs aren't allowed. And while there aren't any picnic tables or grassy areas to stop at along the route, you'll come across some low cement walls where you can sit to rest and enjoy a snack. On the northeastern stretch, for just over half a mile, the path converges with the road and you'll share it with passing cars; there are some sidewalks along the stretch, but stay mindful of traffic.

Connect with . . .

3 Feast on famous chicken in Hollywood

7 Find Griffith Park's hidden gems

35 Go international bakery-hopping in East Hollywood

26 Enjoy the cultural feast of the Piñata District

Neighborhoods and City Streets • Food and Drink • Shopping • For All Ages

Why Go: Come for a kid-friendly party atmosphere, with a treasure trove of Latin American goods—including, yes, piñatas—and a bustling street food scene.

Where: Downtown on E. Olympic Blvd. from Stanford Ave. to S. Central Ave. • Metro bus 53 to Central/Olympic or 66 to Central/Olympic or 9th/Stanford

Timing: For the ultimate sidewalk fiesta, visit on the weekend and block off at least three hours. Stores and street vendors generally open as early as 7am and close by 7pm.

A large, multicolored papier-mâché turtle that was too precious to destroy at my wedding shower. A wide-brimmed cowboy hat, two donkeys, and a tall pink number with white polka dots—all among an assortment of creations purchased for my daughter's first birthday. Beautiful piñatas made here in the heart of L.A. have marked big moments in my family's life. The turtle "lived" for six long years, and "pink-and-white-polka-dotted #1" remains intact in our hallway closet nearly a decade later.

If your party calls for a piñata—and really, shouldn't they all?—you'd be cheating yourself out of a memorable outing by not getting one at the Piñata District. The approximately half-mile block of **Olympic Boulevard** has piñatas of all sizes, for all ages and practically every occasion. And for some, a visit here may feel like you've taken a trip to our southern neighbor without crossing the border. My goddaughter, Veronica—who had not been to the district since she was a kid and had just returned from a trip to her *abuela*'s ancestral home in Tlaquepaque, Jalisco—excitedly exclaimed upon arrival, "It's like a little Mexico!"

A good starting point in the Piñata District is **Navarro's Party Supply** (1258 E. Olympic Blvd., #B, C, D, 213/488-1184), at the corridor's southeastern end; it has its own parking lot and offers lots to explore. Outside the store, loads of fresh produce is available. Inside, the ceiling is full of hanging piñatas—ranging from princesses and video game characters to oversized gold- and silver-wrapped beer bottles—and party supplies (including my favorite,

colorful pottery for sale

Navarro's Party Supply

candy and more candy

grill at Quesadillas "Lucy

confetti cannons). Veronica was happy to see aisle upon aisle of candies and chocolates from Mexico, including De la Rosa Mazapán, a family favorite, and multicolored coconut candy from Tlaquepaque available in bulk. You could easily spend an hour in this one shop.

Take a left as you exit Navarro's and continue northwest up Olympic, where the district's festive and immersive sidewalk corridor begins. It's hard to discern where one store or stall starts or stops. Shops along the way are filled with product-packed aisles. Arrays of piñatas with colorful streamers, inflatable toys, and *papel picado* (decorative, intricately cut sheets of paper) hang overhead. Towering multicolored umbrellas shade tables of more goods for sale outdoors. Street food vendors dish tasty delicacies you can consume beneath their pop-up canopies as music blasts from their radios.

At **Tapia's Party Supplies** (1248 E. Olympic Blvd., 213/488-1123), next door to Navarro's, you'll find adult-oriented piñatas in shapes that will make you blush or laugh; for example, the man and woman in their birthday suits with exaggerated protruding features, which an employee told me are popular for bachelor and bachelorette parties. When I asked her what young kids are buying these days, she said without pausing, "CoComelon," particularly in the form of watermelon TV piñatas modeled after the logo of the animated kids' show. At Tapia's, you'll also be drawn to the selection of pottery, including pitchers, plates, and painted vases, perfect to gift or dress up your home. Nearby, at **Fiesta Mex** (1246 E. Olympic Blvd., 213/622-2446), you'll enjoy perusing a large selection of dried chiles, stacked nearly three feet high, as well as dried mango and chewy candies in a variety of flavors available by the scoop.

Aside from its party-supply stores, the Piñata District is known for its freshly prepared food, with sidewalk carts and grills that lure with enticing aromas, such as **Tacos El Chivo** (1283 E. Olympic Blvd., 323/898-3063) with its mega-sized *al pastor* (pork) on a rotating spit. Next to it is popular sweets destination **Raquel's Candy 'N' Confections** (1238 E. Olympic Blvd., 213/327-0802, www.raquelscnc.com). **Quesadillas "Lucy"** (1239 E. Olympic Blvd., 213/505-6424) sates specific cravings with items like a bacon-wrapped hot dog, *pupusa queso con frijoles* (thick corn tortilla stuffed with beans and cheese), and *huitlacoche y pastor mulita* (quesadilla with corn fungus and marinated pork), and you can enjoy your selections on the shaded outdoor seating area with long tables perfect for big groups. Also keep an eye out for cowboy hat-wearing, longtime sidewalk fixture **Candelario Padilla** grilling *elotes* (Mexican street corn) among other vendors specializing in delicacies such as churros and chicharrónes.

Vendors also push their wares and culinary offerings all along Olympic. One regular greeted us with a joke, then handed us his business card with a picture of him in full clown regalia, saying he's available for hire. You never know what you'll find!

You'll need cash to enjoy much of the Piñata District's offerings, but there are ATMs in the area. One other essential: Behind Quesadillas "Lucy," past Raquel's Candy 'N' Confections' side entrance, look for the bright yellow-and-red-painted sandwich board exclaiming, "Restrooms: Baños Publicos $3," sure to be a welcome sight after you've downed a large horchata or agua fresca

Connect with . . .

🅱 Buy fresh blooms in the Flower District
🅱 Tour Downtown architecture
🅱 Browse antique and architectural salvage stores

27 **Check out the L.A. jazz scene**

Entertainment and Events • Art and Culture

Why Go: Enjoy a variety of experiences at the city's lively jazz clubs.

Where: Citywide

Timing: Find venues' respective calendars online.

While L.A. isn't the first place that comes to mind when people think of major U.S. jazz scenes, the musical form has a rich history here. From the 1920s to the 1950s, South L.A.'s Central Avenue was home to numerous jazz clubs that attracted people near and far to see such icons as Jelly Roll Morton, Billie Holiday, Duke Ellington, Gerald Wilson, and Charles Mingus. Today, jazz venues are found all over the city, with some gems tucked away, and fans can catch shows nearly every day of the week. I'm a casual jazz listener, not a connoisseur, but as a starting point, here are a few venues that offer distinctly different ways to experience the local scene, which is as varied as our neighborhoods.

Cofounded by poet and activist Kamau Daáood and the late jazz drummer Billy Higgins, educational and performance venue **The World Stage** (4321 Degnan Blvd., 323/293-2451, www.theworldstage.org) has been going strong in Leimert Park, the heart of L.A.'s African American community, since 1989. It hosts jazz shows (from $20) featuring local and visiting musicians two nights a week, generally Friday and Saturday. The intimate, no-frills space has a capacity of 100 and is open to music lovers of all ages. I also highly recommend attending the Billy Higgins Instrumental Jam Session (8pm-11pm Thurs.) and Rose Gales Vocal Jam Session (8pm-11pm Sun.). It's a $5 donation for either at the door—that being the back door; you enter the venue through the rear alley that runs parallel to Degnan. Just follow the music. Musicians and vocalists who are versed in jazz standards are welcome to sign up to participate in the lively sessions upon arrival; during the show, the host calls people off the list to perform two songs. The format makes for the coolest experience, particularly on the Billy Higgins night, when you get to see one-night-only combinations of musicians

1: Amber Weekes and Richard Simon performing at the Catalina Jazz Club **2:** "Mike the Barber" at The World Stage **3:** Ethan Chilton and The Planets ensemble at Sam First **4:** inside The World Stage who have never performed together before. There are typically five musicians on stage who get swapped out over the course of the evening, and you never know what magic might take place as each unique ensemble creates its layered sound, takes turns on solos, and develops camaraderie—backed by the supportive hollering from the crowd and fellow musicians. Note there's no bar or alcohol served at The World Stage; here, it's all about the music, and the energy is infectious.

Over in Hollywood, the **Catalina Jazz Club** (6725 Sunset Blvd., 323/466-2210, www.catalinajazzclub.com), named for its owner, Catalina Popescu, opened in 1986 with Dizzy Gillespie as its first act at its original location on Cahuenga Boulevard. The club is now located on the bottom floor of an office building; enter via the main lobby, where a security guard will lead you to the club's marked door in the back, or via the rear parking lot and through the building's outdoor patio. The all-ages club offers old-school, sit-down, tablecloth dining and entertainment at its very best, with the lights turned down low, bright spotlights on the performers, and a mellow, admiring crowd. Seating is first-come, first-served and accommodates upward of 250 people, spread out around the raised, red-curtained stage. Drop-ins are generally fine, but for big names coming through—such as veteran and award-winning jazz acts like conguero and singer Poncho Sanchez, vocalist Lisa Fischer, and legendary composer Chick Corea—purchase tickets (from $25) in advance online. Be prepared for the additional charge of dinner or a two-drink minimum per person, common to L.A. jazz clubs.

Conveniently located next to LAX for traveling acts and Westsiders—but worth the drive for jazz lovers—is **Sam First** (6171 W. Century Blvd. #180, 424/800-2006, www.samfirstbar.com), a 21-and-over club that puts musicians as close to the audience as it gets, with seating limited to 30 people. Artists perform in a corner of the bar at the same level as the audience, as if you're hosting them in your own living room—an intimate quality that makes it particularly appealing to performers and fans alike. Opened in 2018 by developer Paul Solomon, the club is named after his grandfather. Sam First's entrance is somewhat hidden from street level, so look for the yellow neon sign with a needle and thread—Solomon's grandfather was a tailor—and "Bar" beneath it. You'll also notice an outdoor patio to chill at before or after the club's shows (7:30pm and 9pm Tues.-Sat., from $20 per set). Sam First's acoustics are much-touted, for good reason; I never noticed the sound of passing planes—but

Central Avenue Jazz Festival

Started in 1996, the two-day **Central Avenue Jazz Festival** (Central Ave., www.centralavejazzfest.com, late July, free) in South L.A. preserves the neighborhood's jazz history. It's held near the legendary **Dunbar Hotel** (4225 S. Central Ave.), which opened in 1928 as the Hotel Somerville and provided first-class lodgings to African Americans in then-segregated L.A., as well as served as a cultural hub for the community, hosting the likes of Louis Armstrong, Bessie Smith, Lena Horne, and Count Basie. Today it provides affordable housing to seniors. During the summer festival, thousands of people of all ages come to the neighborhood to catch performances by West Coast jazz artists on outdoor stages, dance in the streets, enjoy food and drink from local vendors, and participate in music and art workshops.

I could hear the bartender stirring ice cubes during a quiet solo with an attentive audience. Past performers here have included pianists and composers Eric Reed and Vardan Ovsepian, bassist Mark Dresser, and vocalist Melissa Morgan. There is seating at the bar, a long central table, and curvy lounge banquettes. Given the limited space, purchase tickets ahead of time to guarantee you'll get in.

28 Eat your way around Asia at specialty markets

Food and Drink • Neighborhoods and City Streets

Why Go: Fill your tummy with freshly prepared Asian dishes and your pantry and fridge with an assortment of goods not found at your standard grocery chains.

Where: Citywide

Timing: Allow an hour to shop and dine at each of these markets. Many are open from morning to late at night, though some on-site eateries close earlier in the day.

As a metropolis with a large population of Asian Americans, L.A. has an abundance of markets catering to specific culinary tastes. This means Angelenos can enjoy authentic ingredients, meals, and goods from other countries without venturing very far. Everyone has their go-to Asian market. As a person who likes to eat but not really cook, my favorites are markets with the added bonus of on-site eateries. Come with an appetite, both for a meal and a willingness to wander each aisle.

For decades, I've frequented the **Little Tokyo Market Place** (333 S. Alameda St. #100, 213/617-0030, www.littletokyomarket.com) in the Little Tokyo Galleria shopping center. In addition to the usual rows of refrigerated tofu and miso varieties and sushi and sashimi to go that you'll find at many Japanese grocery stores, there's a section for *senbei* (rice crackers) and *monaka* (sweets), a refrigerated display dedicated to mushrooms (from enoki to king trumpet to oyster), and tanks of live seafood, including abalone and crabs. I come for items like packs of udon and soba noodles, imported Morinaga caramels, and Koda Farms' *mochiko* flour (for making desserts). Prepared food options, which you can eat in the grocery store's sizable dining area near the entrance, include **Sakura Noodle,** which offers curry, udon, soba, ramen, and teriyaki dishes, and **Oh My Poki,** where you choose your fish, the form it'll take (bowl, salad, nacho, wrap), the spice level, toppings, and a side.

At Koreatown's spacious **California Market** (450 S. Western Ave., 213/382-9444, www.gajumarketplace.com), peruse the various types of kimchi and, if you're a fan of Kore-

▲ kimchi at California Market

▲ fish at Seafood City Supermarket

▲ Little Tokyo Market Place

131

an dramas and K-pop, keep an eye out for South Korean celebrities on food packaging (I see you, Park Seo-joon). I also highly recommend choosing from the wide selection of frozen dumplings and picking up a stacked bamboo steamer here while you're at it so you can prepare them to perfection. Or get some precut or seasoned meat (there's so much!) and, if you want to do it up, buy a Korean-style barbecue grill so you can cook it on your dining table. I'm always charmed to receive a choice of a free bottle of hand soap or a pack of sanitizing wipes (for purchases of $100 or more). For on-site dining, **California Market Gimbap** offers traditional Korean favorites such as dried pollack soup and *kimbap* (Korean sushi rolls). Also in the market is an outpost of Korea's popular **Twozone Chicken,** where you choose from 11 types of sauces for your chicken—the most popular being the #2 (sweet, sour, and spicy) and #3 (soy garlic). For something sweet, pick up Asian, French, and American pastries and breads at **Tous les Jours,** a well-known South Korean bakery chain.

Just a quick drive east is the Little Bangladesh-adjacent **Aladin Sweets & Market** (139 S. Vermont Ave., 213/382-9592, http://aladin-sweets-market-inc.square.site), which has

▲ prepared foods at Aladin Sweets & Market

been serving L.A.'s South Asian community since the mid-1980s. Aladin is the smallest market on this list and likely takes up just 10 percent of the square footage of the others, but it packs a flavorful punch. It has a handful of heavily stocked aisles that include essential spices, traditional Indian recipe mixes, *kadai* (cauldron) cooking pans, and freezers full of halal meats and imported fish. From the market's hot food counter, you can order traditional Bangladeshi cuisine, including kababs, curries (the fish is popular), and rice dishes, then enjoy in one of the groovy, patterned vinyl booths in the dedicated dining area. There are 21 types of bite-sized Indian sweets (from the cheese-based *kacha gulla* to the oval-shaped *chom chom*) to choose from for dessert.

Because of the sizable FilAm community you'll encounter at the Eagle Rock Plaza mall and its many Filipino businesses, I refer to it as "Greenhills" after a popular shopping destination I love visiting in Metro Manila. One of these is **Seafood City Supermarket** (2700 Colorado Blvd., Ste. #140, 323/543-2660, www.seafoodcity.com), a SoCal-founded Filipino grocery chain. Rows of ice-packed cases in the market are stacked high with fish, shrimp, and other seafood; you can pick up precooked fish trays to take home, or make your seafood selection and take advantage of the free frying service often found at Filipino markets. Enjoy Tagalog songs playing over the speakers while you browse the produce aisle, with items like bitter melon, *talong* (Filipino eggplant), and boxes of mangoes. There are also large sections of *longanisa* (sausages), bottles of fish and banana sauces, and *bagoong* (shrimp paste)—items always on my family's shopping list. The supermarket has a "street food" counter, too, with items like *okoy* (shrimp fritters) and fried lobster balls, but you may be more tempted by Seafood City's fast-food eatery, **Crispy Town,** popular for its *chicaron bulaklak* (deep-fried chicken skins) and fried smelt.

29 Learn some new moves at Dance DTLA

Entertainment and Events • For All Ages

Why Go: L.A.'s Music Center is one of the city's most iconic performing art venues and offers the biggest and friendliest dance class you'll experience in the city, gratis.

Where: Jerry Moss Plaza at the Music Center • 135 N. Grand Ave. • Metro B Line (Red) to Civic Center/Grand Park Station • Metro bus 60 or LADOT DASH B bus to Grand Ave./1st St.

Timing: Dance DTLA takes place on summer Fridays 7pm-11pm, with 5-8 events scheduled over the season. Arrive on time to catch the first lesson; additional instructions are given throughout the night.

Whether you're a beginner or a pro, you'll want to experience the **Music Center's Dance DTLA** (213/972-7211, www.musiccenter.org/dancedtla, free), when the **Jerry Moss Plaza** becomes the ultimate outdoor club for the whole community. People of all ages and abilities are invited to themed dance evenings during this summer series that includes lessons on a specific style of dance, from Motown and disco to Bollywood and K-pop. A friendly dance instructor, accompanied onstage by an American Sign Language interpreter, and a live DJ host the night's festivities. A mega-sized wooden dance floor is set up, and big screens on either side of a raised stage broadcast the instructor as well as action on the floor, so it's easy to follow along wherever you are on the plaza.

My preferred way to enter the Jerry Moss Plaza is via street level at Grand Avenue, directly across from Grand Park's Arthur J. Will Memorial Fountain (which is always worth a visit at night, lit in colorful fashion that dramatizes the spectacular tiered design and harmonized water show). Either proceed up the escalator to the plaza level or, better yet, ascend via the wide lighted staircase; it'll make you feel like you're on a Vegas stage.

On the dance floor you'll find Angelenos from practically every walk of life, from Downtown workers to parents with kids to people with walkers. The night kicks off with the in-

the lighted steps leading to Jerry Moss Plaza

a refreshing fruit cup to enjoy between dancing

Dance DTLA's Motown Night in Jerry Moss Plaza

▲ the Music Center on Dance DTLA night

structor breaking dances down into simple moves to build on, and then showing how to connect the moves into combinations. There's nothing quite like dancing in unison with throngs of strangers to make you love a summer night even more, as smiles and bodies blanket the plaza. You'll be making friends with your dancing neighbors in no time. Over the course of the evening there are periodic dance instruction segments, and DJs spin music for free-dance sessions.

The spacious plaza is beautifully lit, with a cascade of colorful changing lights streaming from the stage railings onto the dance floor, on either side of which are plenty of tables at which to lounge or eat (plus people dancing in between). If you're looking for a refreshment, I highly recommend getting a large fruit cup with fresh-squeezed lime and Tajín seasoning from the cart parked in front of the adjacent **Mark Taper Forum.** If you like it with a kick, ask to top it off with *chamoy* sauce (a spicy condiment made from fruit and flavored with chiles). This is also a nice area for a respite from the crowds, with the glistening shallow pools that surround the Mark Taper Forum looking especially nice at night. Conveniently

136

nearby are some of the fanciest modern public restrooms in the city, cutely named a "tinkle-torium."

For other food and beverages, there's **The Mullin Wine Bar** (http://themullinla.com) on-site, serving a selection of wine and craft cocktails, as well as burgers and chips, near the Grand Avenue staircase. A few food trucks also park near the plaza entrance on Hope Street.

Come solo, the crowd is friendly! Or make it a date night or family outing that you won't forget. Put on your favorite dance shoes and outfit, or dress to match the theme for the evening. The energy is infectious, so just have fun and embrace the moment. The best part is the amazing feeling you'll get dancing with an excited crowd of a thousand Angelenos—and you can experience it again and again throughout the season, acquiring new dance moves along the way.

Connect with . . .
8 Sample late-night tacos on Sunset Boulevard

30 Find unexpected art and culture in L.A.'s cemeteries

Iconic L.A. • Art and Culture

Why Go: Our city's cemeteries have unique offerings for the living.

Where: Citywide

Timing: Visit cemetery websites for hours and events.

A cemetery isn't generally where one would think to venture for a day or night out on the town. But in Los Angeles, many burial grounds go above and beyond providing loved ones with final resting places.

No cemetery can compare to **Hollywood Forever** (6000 Santa Monica Blvd., 323/784-7679, http://hollywoodforever.com) in terms of breadth of cultural offerings and celebrities interred on its glorious grounds. Founded in 1899, the cemetery is home to Judy Garland, Rudolph Valentino, Estelle Getty, Burt Reynolds, Cecil B. DeMille, John Huston, Bugsy Siegel, and Dee Dee and Johnny Ramone—whose four-foot-high bronze statue serves as grave marker. If you'd like a guide, you can book **The Cemetery of the Stars** walking tour (www.cemeterytour.com, 2.5 hours, Sat.). But Hollywood Forever also doubles as a cultural venue (prices vary). It programs outdoor concerts in summer and indoor concerts year-round at its **Masonic Lodge,** hosting acts like Karen O, Chvrches, Ana Tijoux, and Miguel with Kendrick Lamar and Snoop Dogg. The cemetery has also hosted literary events featuring Roxane Gay and Joyce Carol Oates. Donation-based yoga classes take place every morning on its Fairbanks Lawn, which is also where you can join hundreds of Angelenos beneath the stars when Hollywood Forever, in partnership with the **Cinespia** film organization, presents outdoor film screenings. Movies have ranged from Hollywood classic *Some Like It Hot* to horror flick *The Shining* to the family-friendly *Muppet Movie*. Another big event at the cemetery is its annual **Día de los Muertos** (www.ladayofthedead.com, Sat. before Nov. 2), touted as the largest of its kind outside of Mexico.

Adjacent to Griffith Park is California's largest Jewish cemetery, **Mount Sinai Memo-**

1: Fernando Aceves's *David Bowie: Among the Mexican Masters* exhibit at Forest Lawn Museum
2: Día de los Muertos at Hollywood Forever
3: Portal of the Folded Wings at Pierce Brothers Valhalla Memorial Park **4:** Johnny Ramone gravestone at Hollywood Forever

rial Park (5950 Forest Lawn Dr., 800/600-0076, http://mountsinaiparks.org), established in the 1950s. Its *Heritage Mosaic* (1984) alone is worth the trip. Enter through the gates at Mount Sinai Drive and follow the road up to see the magnificent 145-foot-long by 30-foot-high masterpiece. Modeled after a painting by L.A. artist Neil Boyle and created with individually cut pieces of Venetian glass—more than 2.5 million in all—it depicts more than 350 years of Jewish life in the United States. View it chronologically from right to left. Scenes cover the arrival of the first Jewish settlers in 1654 and a garment labor strike in New York in 1909—an event in which 20,000-plus Jewish immigrants participated—as well as images of Jewish American trailblazers such as Jonas Salk, the physician and researcher who developed the polio vaccine; clothing manufacturer Levi Strauss; and poet Emma Lazarus.

A very different sort of tribute is at the **Pierce Brothers Valhalla Memorial Park** (10621 Victory Blvd., 818/763-9121, www.dignitymemorial.com), situated near Burbank—where Lockheed had aircraft manufacturing plants for 60 years and the Hollywood Burbank Airport is based. Designed in 1924 by sculptor Federico Giorgi and architect Kenneth J. MacDonald Jr., the cemetery's extraordinary Mission-style rotunda stands 75 feet tall and is made of marble, cement, and mosaic; its size and design are far removed from the commercial buildings and suburban tract housing surrounding the grounds. To find the ornately designed shrine, enter via Valhalla Drive. Led by local aviation enthusiast James Gillette, the structure in later years was reimagined as a shrine to aviation, dedicated as the **Portal of the Folded Wings** on the 50th anniversary of the first powered flight, in December 1953. Standing beneath it, you can fittingly hear the sounds of planes departing and landing on the airport runway nearby. Some might find the shrine gaudy or odd, especially with the addition of a space shuttle replica donated from the movie *Armageddon,* placed in front of it to memorialize those who perished in the *Columbia* shuttle. To me, though, this site couldn't be more Los Angeles. Where else can you find Spanish Colonial Revival architecture juxtaposed with a Hollywood prop to honor lives lost? On the stone-slab floor beneath the rotunda are the grave markers of aviation pioneers, historians, and designers, whose ashes are interred below. And three of the shrine's four corner rooms collectively house what is perhaps the smallest aviation museum in the country—the volunteer-run **Burbank Aviation**

Museum, open the first Sunday of the month, which documents the city's aviation history through model planes, archival images, and other memorabilia.

One of my favorite cemeteries to visit is one that many in the city can see from afar—only they don't realize the white building with a large cross high atop the hill is also a site where significant artworks and exhibits can be found. Glendale's **Forest Lawn** (1712 S. Glendale Ave., 323/254-1313, http://forestlawn.com) opened in 1906, and many legends are buried here: Elizabeth Taylor, Nat King Cole, Clark Gable, Dorothy Dandridge, Humphrey Bogart, Walt Disney, Michael Jackson, and Sammy Davis Jr. among them. Numerous reproductions of famous art are also on the cemetery's grounds, including full-size marble reproductions of Michelangelo's *David* and Thorvaldsen's *Christus,* both located near the top of the hill on Cathedral Drive. Following the road until it ends brings you to the modest-sized **Forest Lawn Museum** (free admission), where I had the pleasure of covering a solo exhibit by Mexican photographer Fernando Aceves, *David Bowie: Among the Mexican Masters,* featuring photos of the icon as he toured cultural sites in Mexico in 1997. Other shows have focused on aerial photography, stained glass, and *Peanuts* comic strips; you never know what to expect! One massive work in the adjoining **Hall of Crucifixion-Resurrection** (free admission) is permanent: Polish artist Jan Styka's *The Crucifixion* (circa early 1900s), supposedly the world's largest religious painting at 195 by 45 feet. Forest Lawn had to construct the hall just to house it, and added several rows of classic red-velvet theater seats as well. Also in the hall, with limited viewing at just 25-minute intervals, is U.S. artist Robert Clark's 70-by-52-foot painting, *The Resurrection* (1965). In keeping with only-in-L.A. oddities, visitors were treated to a viewing of the *Peanuts* movie during that exhibit's run—on a screen in front of the curtained *Crucifixion.*

Connect with . . .
㉑ Celebrate life and death during Día de los Muertos

31 Stroll around the Venice Canals

Get Outside • Neighborhoods and City Streets • For All Ages

Why Go: It's fun to play tourist with a walk along these tranquil waterways.

Where: Between S. Venice Blvd. and 28th Ave., Strongs Dr. and Eastern Ct. • Metro bus 33 to Venice Way/Riviera or Culver CityBus Line 1 to Pacific Ave./S. Venice Blvd.

Timing: Plan to spend an hour here.

All too often locals dismiss what's considered touristy. While I've frequented Venice's boardwalk over the years, it took a friend visiting from Montreal asking to see the canals to get me to visit them as an adult, and they have a fascinating history. The neighborhood's founder, developer Abbot Kinney, opened his grand "Venice of America" in 1905, modeling buildings after the Italian city's architecture and creating his version of its canals. The Venice Canals were constructed from existing saltwater marshlands—initially with the help of mule teams, then steam shovels that could work faster. The original seven canals covered almost two miles, surrounding four islands. Pedestrian foot traffic and waterway traffic were prioritized. Residents navigated the canals in boats or canoes, and tourists enjoyed gondola rides while being serenaded. Another set of smaller canals were later added south of the original ones, connecting via a mile-long Grand Canal, and these Short Line Canals, each about 50 feet wide, are what you can still walk along today (though gone are the gondola rides); the original canals were filled in starting in 1929 and paved to make way for cars.

It's easy to navigate the existing canals because they're laid out in a grid. Finding parking in the area is much trickier (you're likelier to luck out on a spot on Venice Boulevard rather than the narrow neighborhood streets immediately surrounding the canals). The long **Grand Canal** to the west runs parallel to the **Eastern Canal** on the other end, and four canals run perpendicular to them: **Carroll, Linnie, Howland,** and **Sherman.**

An easy entry point is Dell Avenue at South Venice Boulevard, as it runs directly through the smaller canals. Note, though, that Dell is the one street that allows car traffic (one-way)

palm tree reflections in a Venice canal

ducks relaxing along the canal

a decorative fence line along a canal pathway

over the canals; the sidewalk on this street is very narrow, and not all drivers travel at the suggested speed limit, so stay mindful. All other canal bridges and sidewalks in the area are for foot traffic only and grant different views of the waterways and tightly packed homes in between.

Let yourself wander. On our visit, we simply followed whatever attracted our attention—a boat, a feathered friend, a cute house. With its peaceful waters, pretty arched pedestrian bridges (nine total), and residential architecture—bungalows, boathouses, and modern glass-heavy square boxes—the scene feels a world away from the packed Venice Boardwalk just a five-minute walk away. Probably much like the thousands of people who visit each year, we thought, "Wouldn't it be nice to live here?"

Linnie Canal Park (200 Linnie Canal) has a swing set and small play structure, friendly for smaller kids, and a smidgen of a green space where you can picnic. In the east corner of the pocket park is a particularly unique feature—a ducks-only area; there's even a small archway in the fence for the fowl to enter from the canals into the grassy area, which has a small pond. Also in the park is a "Meet Our Migratory Birds" poster to help you identify some of the species you might spot on your stroll, like the double-crested cormorant, red-breasted merganser, and red-tailed hawk. On the corner of the Grand Canal and Carroll Canal pathway, look for the large tree next to the floating dock, with its free little library stand and welcoming bench to take a reading break. You may find other amusements in the backyards of various residents (a flamingo fence line, someone playing an instrument on their patio).

Special **canal events** over the years have included row-in movie nights, July 4th festivities, and a winter holiday parade featuring boats bedecked in lights. Swimming isn't permitted, but you can bring your own nonmotorized watercraft, such as paddleboards and kayaks, into the canals between 9am and 6pm.

32 Relax and refresh at a 24-hour Korean spa

Why Go: Steam, soak, and enjoy other self-care services for surprisingly affordable rates.

Where: Westlake neighborhood

Timing: A standard entry fee allows you to enjoy these spas for the whole day, with an additional fee for an overnight stay. Drop in any time, but book spa services online at least two weeks in advance.

For years my girlfriends have raved about ***jimjilbangs***—South Korean-style bathhouses—preferring them to familiar chains or hotel spas for their affordability and laidback environments, as well as their multigenerational appeal. Los Angeles, which is home to the largest Korean American population in the country, has a number of these spas. My only experience with *jimjilbangs* was seeing them in K-dramas, in which they regularly serve as settings, but after hearing about them for so long I decided I had to give them a try. Believe the K-spa hype!

Jimjilbangs generally operate continuously and are microworlds unto themselves, designed to be places for refreshing and whiling away a day with family or friends. Two of the most popular 24-hour Korean spas in L.A. are located less than a mile apart, just east of Koreatown in the Westlake neighborhood. Comparable in their range of offerings, they each include *jimjilbang* standards: coed sauna areas—the centerpiece of the experience—and other common rooms for relaxing and sleeping; gender-separated spa areas with lockers and showers, cold and hot pools, and saunas; and facial and body treatments for additional fees. Both have a general adult admission fee of $30 (waived if you book spa services that meet a minimum dollar amount) that comfortably affords you a seven-hour or longer stay depending on your arrival time, and allow overnight stays for an additional fee. Don't let the

Wı Spa

Spa Palace

spas' dull office building exteriors discourage you; what greets you through their doors is splendor.

Wi Spa (2700 Wilshire Blvd., 213/487-2700, www.wispausa.com) is the most well-known of L.A.'s Korean spas. Fans of late-night talk show *Conan* got a taste of Wi and the *jim-jilbang* experience when host Conan O'Brien, accompanied by actor Steven Yuen, got a crash course in Korean spa etiquette for a segment that went viral. The impressive 48,000-square-foot facility has multiple floors and, as an all-ages spa, is your best bet for a family-friendly atmosphere. The main attraction here is the coed floor, with five beautifully designed saunas. It's like an amusement park for the body, without the lines, with each room designed to benefit the body and skin in specific ways. Here you can easily spot the wide-eyed, curious new visitors versus the regulars casually hanging out like it's their second home. I enjoyed the Clay Sauna the most, burying myself in clay balls known for their medicinal benefits and imported from Korea. The hottest sauna is the dome-shaped, 231-degree Bulgama Room, where you'll sweat out toxins and relax your muscles in no time. You can cool down in the Ice Sauna for the ultimate renewal. The other star of the show at Wi Spa is the must-visit rooftop deck, with cushioned lounge areas amid potted plants and awesome views of historic buildings in the surrounding neighborhood. It's especially stunning at night with its string lights; you'll feel like you're on vacation or living the urban dream. While at Wi, you can also work out in a coed gym, enjoy items like a sausage kimchi stew or fried dumplings at the on-site restaurant, or flip through a book or comic from its library while lounging on a massage chair. If you have kids in tow, you can let them loose on a small play structure.

At **Spa Palace** (620 Union Ave., 213/637-0000, http://spapalacela.com), knight statues in full armor stand guard just beyond the entrance turnstiles, which instantly piques curiosity—it feels surprisingly wacky for a spa, and so L.A., and is indicative of its more eclectic aesthetic. Open to ages 12 and over only, Spa Palace appeals to adults who want an experience without young kids running about. In the large coed common area, six saunas feature live digital temperature readings above their carved, centuries-old-looking wood doors. In the magnificent detoxifying Himalayan Salt room, grab a mat and lie on top of the salt-covered floor to relax your muscles. In the Loess Soil Room, bury yourself in the floor of loess balls for improved blood circulation, and let its earthy smell transport you. Another of Spa

Palace's most prized amenities is its massive coed indoor swimming pool—colorfully lit like a dance club at night. There's a hot tub and smaller wading pool with a rock-wall waterfall, as well as the Aqua Bar, which serves alcohol. The spa also has a restaurant that serves items like bulgogi and spicy soup and noodle dishes, a juice bar, a kids' play area, and a terraced outdoor space with a small waterfall.

When you arrive at either facility, let the front desk know if it's your first time and they'll give you an overview of their layout and services. Attendants provide you with an electronic wristwatch key that gives locker access and lets you purchase food or other services, which you'll pay for when you exit. Towels and drinking water are provided. I suggest bringing your own flip-flops for the wet areas. Basic etiquette at *jimjilbangs* requires showering before entering the pools or saunas, and doing this in the nude is standard (bathing suits aren't allowed). In the clearly designated coed common areas, you'll wear the spa-provided uniform of T-shirts and shorts. Be respectful of people's privacy and refrain from taking any photos inside the locker rooms and spa areas.

Connect with . . .

28 Eat your way around Asia at specialty markets

33 Dance while you browse at Crenshaw Mall's Saturday markets

Entertainment and Events • Shopping • Food and Drink

Why Go: Baldwin Hills Crenshaw Plaza hosts two markets offering great community atmosphere—with a live DJ spinning—while supporting local farms, eateries, and Black entrepreneurs.

Where: Baldwin Hills Crenshaw Plaza, on the promenade and thoroughfare between the mall parking lot and Cinemark at 4020 Marlton Ave. • Metro bus 105 to Marlton/Martin Luther King Jr. or Martin Luther King Jr./Crenshaw

Timing: Crenshaw Farmers' Market is held every Saturday, and Nothing But B.L.K. Flea tends to take place two Saturdays a month—check their Instagram (@nothing butblk) for updates. Time your visit for a weekend when both are scheduled.

The **Baldwin Hills Crenshaw Plaza** (3650 W. Martin Luther King Jr. Blvd, 323/290-6636, www.baldwinhillscrenshawplaza.com), or **Crenshaw Mall** as locals call it, is an important commercial corridor and gathering place for the surrounding neighborhoods of Baldwin Hills and Crenshaw as well as Leimert Park and View Park-Windsor Hills, which have large Black communities. With the city's long history of displacement and lack of investment in Black neighborhoods, residents have organized to preserve and increase Black-owned businesses in the area and ensure stores provide services and products that serve the needs and interests of the neighborhoods' largest demographic. Two Saturday markets held on the mall's spacious, palm-tree-bedecked outdoor promenade and parallel thoroughfare work to do this in celebratory ways, bringing people together in an upbeat atmosphere. You'll hear the live DJ spinning sounds even before you even see the welcoming scene with its many pop-up tents.

The **Crenshaw Farmers' Market** (323/463-3171, http://seela.org/markets-crenshaw, 10am-3pm Sat.) is one of six markets run by Sustainable Economic Enterprises of Los Angeles (SEE-LA) and features more than 20 booths to shop: farm vendors and other produce vendors, prepared food vendors, and local artisans. Check out the produce selection from

1: lunch combo from Caribbean Gourmet
2: Fulaba founder Haby Barry at her booth
3: Lé Trois Apothecary booth **4:** Baldwin Hill
Crenshaw Plaza's promenade on a Saturday

Riverside's **I & M Castellanos Farm,** get eggs from Kern County's **Don Beto's Farms,** and take home locally made honey from Bellflower's **Aunt Willie's Apiary.** On the Saturday I visited with friends and their kids, we enjoyed a bean-and-cheese offering from **Delmy's Pupusas,** a Guyanese platter of curry chicken, rice, and cabbage from **Caribbean Gourmet,** and vegan cookies from **Selah.** We also tried bottles of **Raw Cane Superjuice** and smoothies from **Polar Bear Kitchen.** Abundant seating is available on the mall's promenade, with benches shaded by trees and other ledges and stools on which to relax, eat comfortably, and people-watch. The market also offers free on-site nutrition and cooking classes throughout the year and, while the focus usually stays on food, there are other events as well; I visited during a month-long bike initiative, with a booth offering free bike repairs led by a group that was also organizing bike rides that day to different spots in the neighborhood. Visit the information booth to learn about upcoming events.

When the farmers' market vendors pack up, there's still time to browse the **Nothing But B.L.K. Flea** (http://nothingbutblk.com, 10am-5pm every other Sat.), which has 35-40

⌃ T-shirts by Bank$teeznthingz for sale at Nothing But B.L.K. Flea

vendors. Although the markets are independently produced, they blend fairly seamlessly. It's the flea market's DJ that sets the party soundtrack for the day and gets you dancing while you browse. (Thank you, Myah Stone, aka DJ Myah Moves, for keeping the energy high.) Nothing But B.L.K. Flea, previously known as Melanin Market LA, was launched by friends Jay Funtila and Kris Hibler-Smith to ensure Black-owned businesses and entrepreneurs have spaces to operate. B.L.K. stands for "business, love, and culture," and its heart is set on cultivating community and prosperity. "The focus is in showing that people within the community are able to sell, able to produce their products, and make an income off them," Funtila said. Most vendors are from SoCal, but some come from as far as the Bay Area's Oakland to participate, and artisans are happy to talk about their work. The range of offerings is vast, and includes South L.A. proud T-shirts inscribed with neighborhoods and hangouts by **Bank\$teeznthingz,** sea moss products by **Axumus,** coal incense and crystal burning vessels by **Lé Trois Apothecary,** hair accessories by **Made for Queens,** and jewelry crafted by West African artisans care of Haby Barry's **Fulaba** (the only other place carrying the line? The Smithsonian!).

Connect with . . .

20 Shop for art and wine in West Adams

27 Check out the L.A. jazz scene (The World Stage)

34 Delve into the world's largest LGBTQ collection at ONE Archives

Art and Culture

Why Go: With more than two million items, ONE allows visitors a chance to see rare historical ephemera and publications chronicling queer life in our country.

Where: 909 W. Adams Blvd., 213/743-1561, http://one.usc.edu • Metro bus 37 to Adams/Severance

Timing: Book an appointment online as a guest at libcal.usc.edu/reserve/one-archives, then drop them an email at askone@usc.edu (at least a week in advance) to schedule a 45-minute tour.

Los Angeles is home to the world's largest repository of lesbian, gay, bisexual, transgender, and queer materials. **ONE National Gay & Lesbian Archives at the USC Libraries** has nearly 30,000 books and monographs, almost 700 archival collections, and 13,000-plus periodicals, ranging from newsletters to newspapers, some international in scope and published in different languages. It also holds archival posters and graphics from major events and protests; FBI surveillance records that chronicle the monitoring of queer populations during the 1950s; ephemera such as menus dating back to 1960 from restaurants that catered to LGBTQ clientele; and behavior modification equipment training manuals (including a wireless shocking device and an automatic desensitizer machine used to try to change sexual orientation).

As part of the University of Southern California, ONE Archives draws students, faculty, independent researchers, and media makers, but it's open and free to the public as well. I only became aware of this incredible resource after attending a party here marking the final issue of the L.A.-based *make/shift* magazine, a feminist publication to which I was a contributor that centered the perspectives of queer, genderqueer, and women of color; the magazine's archive now lives among others at ONE.

Check in upon arrival at the two-story building. This is a research institution, so you'll need to follow some basic guidelines during your visit, as well as register as an independent researcher (it takes just a few minutes to do so) to pull items from the collection. Bring your

the first issue of *The Advocate* from September 1967

covers of lesbian publications in the archives

first floor of ONE Archives

ID so you can request items to view after your tour. Both archivists I met there stressed, "This isn't a tourist attraction"—but it is no doubt a national treasure.

On the tour, an archivist will give you an overview of ONE Archives and its history, and then take you behind many closed doors where you'll see a sampling of archival material. Feel free to ask to see specific items: the first issues of Andy Warhol's *Interview* magazine, perhaps? Or maybe something more obscure, such as an 18th-century European monograph discussing homosexuality. Hanging from some bookcases are publications and printed materials in plastic sleeves for quick browsing, from men's fashion catalogs from the late 1960s and '70s to the first issue of *The Advocate* from 1967 (making it the longest-running gay publication in the country)—then called *The Los Angeles Advocate* and selling for just 25 cents.

I particularly enjoyed looking at the collection of matchbooks from bars, clubs, restaurants, and other businesses frequented by the queer community (Coll2010-0409, if you're interested). My guide, reference and instruction librarian Michael D. Oliveira, mentioned that matchbooks are often the only remaining records of places and their locations. As I

ONE Gallery

Another way to experience ONE Archives' vast collections is by visiting its off-site **ONE Gallery** (626 N. Robertson Blvd., 323/698-0410, www.onearchives.org) in West Hollywood. Exhibits are developed in collaboration with the independently run ONE Archives Foundation using or inspired by material from the archives. The foundation also produces free pop-up shows in public spaces, such as building exteriors or on fences, which can take the form of archival and new posters centering the LGBTQ community.

looked through a binder from Southern California, it was fun to see the names of venues I've visited with friends, like the gently used vintage black matchbook for the WeHo dive bar Spike on Santa Monica Boulevard, or one for the now-shuttered Video West, bearing its awesome pink retro script. It makes you thankful that these pieces of history have a home that you can return to again.

Other notable items among the archives' collection include first editions and rare books by celebrated authors such as Armistead Maupin and James Baldwin; photography, oral history, and chapbooks by poet, writer, and activist Audre Lorde; lesbian publications including *The Ladder, Dyke, The Lesbian Tide, Off Our Backs,* and *Vice Versa: America's Gayest Magazine*—believed to be the first lesbian publication, produced in DIY fashion in L.A. in 1947; and materials from the Mattachine Society, an early gay rights organization that started in L.A. in 1951 to secretly publish *ONE Magazine* (from which the archives' name originates)—the first U.S. publication for homosexuals to be distributed widely.

ONE Archives also hosts a variety of public events throughout the year, including art openings, book signings, performances, and themed talks featuring artists whose work has been influenced by the library's collection.

Connect with . . .
20 Shop for art and wine in West Adams
39 Browse antique and architectural salvage shops
40 Savor L.A.'s multicultural flavors at celebrated family-run eateries (Mercado la Paloma)

35 Go international bakery-hopping in East Hollywood

Food and Drink • Neighborhoods and City Streets

Why Go: Sample the flavors of numerous countries—from the Philippines to El Salvador to Armenia—along a mile-long stretch of Santa Monica Boulevard.

Where: Santa Monica Blvd. from N. Serrano Ave. to N. Madison Ave. • Metro bus 4 to Santa Monica/Hobart (western end) or Santa Monica/Madison (eastern end)

Timing: For the freshest and largest variety of offerings, embark on your bakery spree in the morning and give yourself a few hours to walk and snack along the way.

When I was a child, East Hollywood was my family's epicenter. It's where our large extended family gathered at my *lolo* and *lola*'s (grandparents') Craftsman house and home to the hospital where my sisters and I were born; Los Angeles City College, where we took recreational classes as kids; and the many Filipino businesses that my family frequented. Asian, Armenian, and Latino immigrant families mostly populate the working-class neighborhood, and on a mile-long stretch of **Santa Monica Boulevard** that cuts through East Hollywood, you can delight in this diversity by treating your taste buds to baked delicacies from around the world. The streetscape, consisting of many weathered storefronts, isn't quite picturesque, but these mostly longstanding, family-owned businesses are beloved, serving staples to the many immigrant residents in the area who want an authentic taste of home.

Start your eating tour—pace yourself and be prepared with shopping bags to hold treats to eat later—at the western end of the stretch, right next to the 101 freeway. It's easy to walk or drive along this route (metered and street parking are available). Tucked in a strip mall is **Café Paris/Hellen Patisserie** (5357 Santa Monica Blvd., 323/464-4500), identifiable by its blue-and-red signage featuring the Eiffel Tower—wonderfully dwarfed by the large palm tree in its charming outdoor patio. Inside is an equally quaint seating area with French bistro chairs. While the bakery offers the expected croissants, éclairs, and fruit tarts, it also

Guatemalteca Bakery

specializes in Armenian and Russian desserts. Ask for recommendations, buy an assortment of baklava, or order a piece of Russian honey cake.

Cross the street and head east to **Sasoun Bakery** (5114 Santa Monica Blvd., 323/661-1868), which offers sweet and savory Middle Eastern and Armenian baked goods, served by owner David Yeretsian with tongs and a smile. Open since 1985, the bakery is named for the area he's from in Western Armenia and has four other locations in the county. Bring home a pack of sweet tahini bread or select a *lahmadjune* (flatbread with meat) or—my favorite—the spinach *beorek* (triangle-shaped pastry).

Continue east one block to busy **Pacific French Bakery** (5060 Santa Monica Blvd., 323/668-9100, www.pacificfrenchbakery.com), open since 1986. It first, as the name suggests, sold French baked goods, but now a variety of breads can be found here—from popular French rolls to *pan de leche* (sweet milk bread) Hawaiian rolls—plus many sweet and savory Latin American offerings. Pick up *pastelitos* (puffed pastries) or a Guatemalan torta with *aucar* (sugar) or *cuerno* (sesame).

▲ Pacific French Bakery

If it's around lunchtime, cross the street and continue east for **DeSano Pizza Bakery** (4959 Santa Monica Blvd., 323/913-7000, www.desanopizza.com). Its pizza is made in traditional Neapolitan style: baked in a wood-burning oven, following Associazione Verace Pizza Napoletana guidelines, and using specific Italian-made ingredients. It's also a fun place to eat, with a spacious dining hall full of picnic tables.

Continue east until you reach the tiny strip mall that's home to **Panderia Salvador-eña Bakery & Deli** (4873 Santa Monica Blvd., 323/666-0219). Order refreshing *charamuscas* (flavored drinks in bags), *pupusas* (thick tortillas stuffed with fillings), or sweet bread and other pan dulce while you catch Spanish-language shows on the overhead TV.

Cross the street and walk another block to **European Baking Co. Inc.** (4800 Santa Monica Blvd., 323/913-0383), where you can order a cake for your next big occasion or bring home a slice just because. It produces eye-catching custom cakes as well as sells some—such as a moist tres leches cake—ready to go.

Another quick walk eastward is the bustling **Guatemalteca Bakery** (4770 Santa Monica Blvd., 323/663-8307). Specializing in Guatemalan fare, it has cases of baked goods, a walk-up counter with a hot food menu, and a large dining area. Choose from an assortment of *panes* (sandwiches), *comidas* (main dishes), and *antojitos* (small dishes). In true L.A. fashion, traditional items like *pacaya* (palm) and *rellenitos* (deep-fried plantains stuffed with refried beans) are offered—but so is chow mein.

Walk east another two blocks to reach your final stop in another strip mall, a Filipino bakery. My family has been visiting the small and dependable **Valerio Family Bakeshop** (4627 Santa Monica Blvd., 323/662-6110) for decades. We love its *ensaymada* (circular sweet bread topped with buttered sugar and shredded cheese), *hopia* (pastry traditionally filled with bean paste), and *shakoy* (twisted donut). On a recent trip, Valerio had run out of many of its baked goods by mid-afternoon (take note), but there was no shortage of bags of *pan de sal* (Filipino bread rolls), thankfully!

Connect with . . .

❼ Find Griffith Park's hidden gems

㉚ Find unexpected art and culture in L.A.'s cemeteries (Hollywood Forever)

36 Get creative with local artisans

Why Go: People of all ages and skill levels are invited to make art in supportive and inspiring environments.

Where: Citywide

Timing: Opportunities are available with these artisans and organizations throughout the year, from public workshops and open studios to private workshops and collaborative art-making events.

There is power in making art together: the potential for personal transformation as you bring something new into being with someone else. I've become acquainted with a number of organizations and artists over the years whose missions and art practices provide people with opportunities to learn their craft in a relaxed setting while fostering a sense of community in the process.

Nonprofit arts program and social enterprise **Piece by Piece** (213/459-1420, www.piecebypiece.org) is responsible for some of the most striking mosaic murals and sculptures in Los Angeles County. You may have seen the organization's exquisite mandalas on the exterior of the Legal Aid Foundation of Los Angeles building (1550 W. 8th St.), the *Water is Life* mural at the Los Angeles County Arboretum and Botanic Garden (301 N. Baldwin Ave., Arcadia), or the 20-foot-long mural along the café counter at Village Well Books & Coffee (9900 Culver City Blvd., Culver City). I learned about the nonprofit after meeting two staff members, Dawn Mendelson and Daniel Villa, at a series of business workshops for artists. Piece by Piece's main mission is to teach and develop artisans by offering free mosaic art workshops, using recycled materials, to low-income and formerly unhoused people with the aim to, in its words, "develop marketable skills, self-confidence, earned income, and an improved quality of life." The general public can volunteer with the group, and my daughter and I did so for a day. The artisans-in-training and teacher artists directed us and talked

Piece by Piece mosaic in process

Concrete Geometric owner Krizia Flores

author with her daughter and artisan John at Piece by Piece in 2018

passionately about their craft and what led them to Piece by Piece. It was amazing to see my then four-year-old kid's little fingers strategically placing discarded shards of tile, glass, and dinnerware into shapes, and her excitement as they emerged as part of a work of art. Months later, the mosaic was placed in an affordable housing community. In addition to volunteer opportunities, Piece by Piece offers pop-up mosaic workshops open to the public and typically free, held at different cultural sites and events in the city throughout the year. Past events have taken place at the annual Central Avenue Jazz Festival (www.centralavejazzfest. com) and the Hauser & Wirth gallery (901 E. 3rd St., www.hauserwirth.com). Visit the website to sign up to volunteer or learn about the next workshop.

Glassell Park is where you'll find the studio of Krizia Flores, the artist behind **Concrete Geometric** (address provided upon booking, 818/359-5325, www.concretegeometric.com), an in-demand line of home decor products and DIY kits. She's known for her stylishly shaped concrete pieces that are multifunctional—we use ours as pen and candle holders or planters—in a range of colors and patterns that instantly bring character to any surface. Learn from her and create a piece of your own by booking a two-hour workshop (individuals $100, groups $75 pp with a minimum of five people). You'll create a piece from start to finish, choosing molds, preparing concrete, selecting and adding color pigments, then pouring and layering it into the molds. There's no need to bring anything except your enthusiasm; Flores provides gloves, an apron, pigments, and molds and generally opens the workshop by asking participants to talk about things or places that inspire them to get them thinking about the design of their piece. Make your session a fun family or friends affair. You could also inquire with Flores about hosting a workshop at your home.

Over in Boyle Heights, a true communal art experience is always in store at the beloved **Self Help Graphics & Art** (1300 E. 1st St., 323/881-6444, www.selfhelpgraphics.com), founded in 1973 by Sister Karen Boccalero and Mexican artists Carlos Bueno and Antonio Ibáñez. An evening I spent here with my daughter and niece years back was especially meaningful; the organization invited the public to a poster-making session before the historic Women's March in 2017, and the space was filled with activists and community members as young as three expressing their feelings and battle cries through text, drawings, and collages. Throughout the year, Angelenos of all ages and abilities interested in printmaking and other

Self Help Graphics & Art's Barrio Mobile Art Studio mural workshop

art forms are invited to attend Self Help's various themed workshops (free–$30)—ranging from tie-dying to papermaking to cyanotype printing—or open printmaking sessions, where you can use the shop's facilities and materials with purchase of a $20 day pass after completing an orientation or attending a workshop by one of its teaching artists. "Having a studio is such a luxury in a city like Los Angeles," shared executive director Betty Avila. "So Self Help becomes kind of a de facto studio space for artists in the community. It is a place that is meant to be open and available and accessible."

37 Steep yourself in the city's teahouse culture

Food and Drink • Art and Culture

Why Go: Enjoy the city's varied range of tea offerings, from artful boba and CBD creations to a modern take on a traditional Chinese tea ceremony.

Where: Citywide

Timing: Give yourself at least an hour to enjoy each of these spots.

Coffeehouses and cafés with distinct personalities and a late-night culture ruled the city during the 1990s, when students, artists, writers, and celebrities alike engaged in long conversations aided by caffeine. Sure, coffee spots are still a big business here, but these days I'm finding more diverse and memorable experiences at the city's teahouses.

For traditional British high tea in a posh setting, visit Downtown's luxurious **Rendez-vous Court** (506 S. Grand Ave., 213/612-1562, www.millenniumhotels.com) in the historic Millennium Biltmore, built in 1922. Here you'll enjoy tea as if you're royalty, with fancy silverware and dinnerware on white tablecloth-covered tables and servers dressed in formal attire. The court itself is a sight to behold, with a marble fountain at its center, plush seating, a baby grand piano, and architectural details—towering archways and a dramatically lit wood ceiling—that will transport you in time. Just as memorable are its organic tea selections, including classics like Earl Grey and Darjeeling, and tiered trays of treats. You can also add Kir Royale or champagne to really up the bill. Afternoon tea is served on the weekends, and reservations are recommended.

At the busy three-story California Market in Koreatown, a different experience awaits—though this spot has a baby grand piano, too—at the top-floor **Ye Stage & Tea** (450 S. Western Ave. #315, 213/400-0309), a teahouse, art gallery, and live music venue, with spacious outdoor and indoor seating areas. It offers traditional Korean teas, including a relaxing barley grass tea, medicinal Ssanghwa tea, and green plum tea, to be enjoyed with an array of dishes, from the prettiest presentation of rice waffles with blueberries and shaved almonds

outdoor seating at Bohemia Tea & Coffee

tea ceremony at Steep LA

tea and side dishes at Ye Stage & Tea

afternoon tea at the Rendezvous Court

bao at Bohemia Tea & Coffee

to the filling and incredibly tasty Pyongyang flat dumplings. The teahouse has intimate spaces created by moveable dividers displaying rotating artwork (available for purchase), as well as something you won't see at most teahouses in L.A.: a Korean *buk* (drum) and brass *jing* (gong) on the stage; live jazz, classical, or Korean music performances take place here at least twice a month.

Near the Sunset Strip is the pleasant **Bohemia Tea & Coffee** (7525 Sunset Blvd., 323/672-8662, http://bohemialosangeles.com), whose interiors hearken to the coffeehouses of the past, with velvet couches, patterned wallpaper, warm lighting, and late-night hours. The scene is mellow in the afternoon and quite packed and lively in the evening, so choose your mood. Bohemia's tea menu is organized into entertaining categories: classics done right, fruity and delightful, and rare and unusual. It also touts the highest grade of matcha from Japan, tea with boba (made fresh each day!), and plentiful milk options (from hemp to macadamia). You can also add CBD to any drink for an additional $3. Sweet and savory treats salute a range of cultures, such as a tikka masala *bao* (a Chinese steamed bun), Armenian flatbread, and Thai tea soft-serve ice cream.

In Chinatown's **Steep LA** (970 N. Broadway St. #112, 213/394-5045, www.steepla. com), located in the courtyard of Mandarin Plaza, you can enjoy a modern take on a traditional Chinese tea ceremony. The teas and teaware are the focus in this bright and modern space, while the knowledgeable and patient staff—including founders Samuel Wang and Lydia Lin—bring (along with their fresh tea) welcomed warmth. First-time visitors will want to ask for recommendations; staff will thoughtfully go over offerings—including black, oolong, green, and pu-erh (fermented) varieties—from the fruitiness of one to the funkiness or floral qualities of another. "We make our teas in-house, when you order," shared Samuel. "We put a lot of time and effort into all our teas, including how much water we put in and at what temperature." And you can taste the difference. On our visit, my daughter and I ran into a couple of friends with their daughter, and they all joined us for the outdoor tea spread—which ended up serving our entire party for an amazingly affordable $20. Along with the Spring Orchid oolong we ordered came some dried mango and guava slivers, and a choice of two pastries; we had an egg tart and sesame seed-topped pastry with shredded pork. I don't want to give away too much about the multistep ceremony—experience it with wonder as we all did the first time—but I'll share some things that stand out: You can choose a cup for the ceremony to match your personality (I went with a hexagonal turquoise cup), the tea spread comes with a small digital timer and directions (including suggested steeping times), and they keep your teapot filled and at a precise temperature on an assigned warmer on the counter. Enjoy the serenity and spectacle of it all.

38 Get a taste of L.A. at Homeboy Bakery and Homegirl Café

Food and Drink • For All Ages

Why Go: Get a behind-the-scenes look at the organization behind the beloved bakery and café that are a part of the world's largest gang-rehabilitation program.

Where: Homeboy Industries •130 W. Bruno St. • 323/526-1254 • http://homeboy-industries.org • Metro L Line (Gold) to Chinatown Station or Metro bus 794, Metro bus 799, or LADOT DASH B to Alameda St./College St.

Timing: Homeboy Industries tours (9am, 11am, and 2pm Mon.-Fri., free) last approximately 30 minutes. Book online 30-90 days in advance. Add on time to dine at the café afterward.

Homeboy Bakery's preservative-free breads and other baked goods—like its colorfully swirled rainbow bread, braided challah, and jalapeño sweet corn baguette—as well as its chips, guacamole, and salsa, are beloved in L.A., found in farmers' markets, stores, and eateries throughout Southern California. What many people don't know is that the bakery is just one of many businesses that are part of a broader social enterprise whose mission is the rehabilitation of former gang members. Founded in Boyle Heights in 1988 by Jesuit priest Father Gregory Boyle, **Homeboy Industries** seeks to provide youth and adult access to education and employment opportunities as an intervention to combat gang violence and high incarceration rates in the city. An estimated 45,000-plus individuals are members of gangs in Los Angeles, which has some 450 active gangs. Various complex social, economic, and personal factors contribute to individuals entering gang life. But there are also thousands of inspiring stories about those who've left. Numerous programs exist in the city and county that aim to support this transition, but Homeboy is arguably the most influential and far-reaching in the world, serving 8,000 people annually. It offers enrollees opportunities to develop job skills through direct work experience in the organization's various ventures, including food production, prep, and service, as well as fields including silkscreen printing and recycling.

Today, free tours of Homeboy's headquarters, now based in Chinatown, offer a unique

Homeboy Industries and Homegirl Café

gift shop merchandise

office of founder Father Gregory Boyle

a meal at Homegirl Café

opportunity to see where the famous bread is baked, and gain a deeper understanding of the organization's workings. A person who has gone through or is currently enrolled in Homeboy's 18-month rehabilitation and reentry program will serve as guide to your small group, which is capped at 12 people. You'll see administrative offices as well as classrooms, where trainees take courses on subjects ranging from college pathways to parenthood. Individual or group therapy sessions, wellness and art classes, and nature outings are also part of Homeboy's rehabilitation program.

Guides invite people to ask questions about the organization, and they may share personal experiences about how they came to be involved. While they're prepared to be asked about almost anything, remember to be considerate. My tour guide was Omar, a veteran of the organization. He was first approached by "G," as Father Boyle is known, when he was just 16 and lived across the street from the original office. "G never gave up on me," he said, even during the times in his life when he felt he wouldn't survive the next day. Omar has been involved off and on with Homeboy since 2007 and leading tours since 2014, explaining how

Homegirl Café

they can be therapeutic for the guides; sharing their stories reminds them of the paths they took to get to where they are now.

Each person you might meet here has a story to tell about the healing process they went through (and continue to go through). A few staff members talked about their journeys with me when I asked, "How long have you been with Homeboy?" Hearing about their struggles, determination, and successes is something I won't soon forget.

Visitors will also be guided through the highly rated on-site **Homegirl Café** and learn about its bakery operations. Cofounded by chef Patricia Zarate, it—like Homeboy Bakery— employs women and men formerly involved in gangs. Many may be familiar with Homegirl even if they've never been to the café; it also runs a successful catering service out of the headquarters, working everything from quinceañeras to corporate galas. Stop here after the tour to enjoy the popular cakes and pies (Omar recommends the red velvet cake) as well as savory dishes. I'd long heard friends rave about the food, so I was excited for my first meal here. The filling *xiliques* (freshly made tortilla chips, beans, salsa rosa, guacamole salsa, and cotija) featured cooked-to-perfection crispy carnitas, and the homemade berry agua fresca was incredible. I also ordered the coffee cake and (of course) took home a loaf of bread.

If you can't make it to the headquarters, Homeboy Industries also runs two other eat- eries in L.A.—City Hall's **Homeboy Diner** (200 N. Spring St., Ste. 210, 213/542-6190) and LAX's **Homeboy Cafe** (400 World Way, Terminal 4, 866/820-1178).

39 Browse antique and architectural salvage shops

Shopping • Neighborhoods and City Streets

Why Go: Three stores on a one-block shopping strip represent L.A. treasure hunting at its best and most convenient.

Where: Downtown on W. 18th St., between S. Grand Ave. and S. Olive St. • Metro bus 38, 55, 78, 79, or 603 to 18th/Olive

Timing: Give yourself a few hours to delve into the smorgasbord at these shops.

The high quality and convenience of a unique trio of antique and architectural salvage stores on a single Downtown block makes this stretch of **18th Street** a perfect destination for people who love items with a history.

When I visited **Vintage Antiques Eclectic** (232 W. 18th St., 213/268-9895), I lucked out on rock star parking right in front; in L.A., that always signals a good day ahead. The shop's goods spill out onto the sidewalk, and on this day included a 1960s wood bar with decoratively etched see-through sliding doors and two bar stools next to a six-foot-high stack of wood chests in various styles and stains. Inside, the packed space holds hundreds of goods both precious (ornate glass decanters) and amusing (a curious number of horse sculptures). If you're looking for a highly curated space, then you've come to the wrong place. But if you're like me, seeing the overwhelming number of items tightly grouped together from floor to ceiling, some in themed sections (clocks, cameras, lamps, silver dinnerware), is thrilling. Whether you're looking for miniature furniture, century-old Persian rugs, or a vintage antler chandelier, you'll find it here. Owner Bob Firooz, who has been in business for nearly a decade (and an antique collector for three), and friend Alex are happy to help guide you in the right direction. When I shared my lifelong love for antique stores with Bob, and that I often dreamed of having my own store someday, he said in all seriousness, "I'll sell it to you." The price tag: "Have the store and everything in it for $250,000." Well, I'm not quite there yet.

Vintage Antiques Eclectic

The Americana Antique Store

Olde Good Things is full of so many good things!

Next door is **The Americana Antique Store** (240 W. 18th St., 213/973-5358, www.theamericanaantique.store), which is family-owned and -run. It moved to this location from Crenshaw Boulevard in Gardena in 2021. Owner Darin Dawson, or "Big D," as he's known, had long dreamed of having a store Downtown, so when he heard from his friends, and now neighbors, Firooz and one of Olde Good Things managers, Paul Blottner, that a space had opened between them, Dawson made that dream a reality. Big D is committed to only selling true vintage items in his store, rather than vintage-inspired goods or antique reproductions. On the day I visited, a traffic light and large collectible American gas sign outside the shop beckoned passersby to enter through two arched doorways, where colorful vintage signage and salvaged restaurant furnishings were thoughtfully staged; it feels like being at a roadside attraction from eras past. I was immediately drawn to a set of four vinyl-cushioned stools decorated as peppermint candy swirls and a large green "Stationery Office Supplies" neon sign from the 1950s. Look up and you'll notice the aluminum foil that lines the shop's sloped ceiling, left by its former tenant (a marijuana grower) to maximize indoor light; it works well with the neon to brighten the space in a spectacular way. If you're here on a hot day, you'll notice that even the fans are several decades old. Insider tip: You can visit to shop as well as sell or trade your own antique finds.

At the end of the block is the 10,000-square-foot, employee-owned **Olde Good Things** (1500 S. Grand Ave., entrance on W. 18th St., 213/746-8600, www.oldegoodthings.com), an L.A. outpost of an architectural salvage store that started in 1995 in New York. Upon entering, you'll be struck by the large and colorful animal statues as well as the hundreds of chandeliers and industrial lighting options. "It's quite the electricity bill," mentioned one employee. The store features six retail zones: furniture, mirrors, hardware, lighting, plumbing, and architectural elements, including ironwork, fences, and gates. You'll also discover things you never knew you wanted: say, a four-foot-tall wood mail sorter with 80 slots still sporting labels with residents' names, or maybe an open-mouthed plaster crocodile. While there are big-ticket items that can run thousands of dollars, you'll also find lower-priced practical items, such as statement doorknobs and the popular antique tin mirrors, as well as interesting wall hooks to instantly bring character to your home. If you're looking to strike a deal on a larger item purchase, the staff may be open to negotiating a price.

lighting and more at Olde Good Things

Inventory at the strip's stores changes often, and if you're on the lookout for something in particular, be sure to let the owners and staff know. Part of the joy of visiting these shops is chatting with them.

Note that these Downtown storefronts run parallel to an overpass of the 10 freeway, with pass-through lanes for buses underneath—so consider taking the bus or, if you're visiting the area by car and it's a weekday, keep a sharp eye out; it's easy to get caught up in the commuter rush and miss the strip.

Connect with . . .

⓭ Buy fresh blooms in the Flower District
㉔ Tour Downtown architecture
㉖ Enjoy the cultural feast of the Piñata District

40 Savor L.A.'s multicultural flavors at celebrated family-run eateries

Food and Drink • Neighborhoods and City Streets

Why Go: From strip-mall eateries to fast-casual counters, these unassuming spots will take your taste buds on a world-class journey.

Where: Citywide

Timing: None of these restaurants take reservations, so if you're coming during the busy lunch or dinner hours, you could encounter a wait—but it'll be worth it.

The more you eat across Los Angeles, the more the city and its myriad cultures open up to you. This is what the late Pulitzer Prize-winning writer **Jonathan Gold**—the only person to receive the award for food criticism—constantly reminded us through his restaurant reviews. Over four decades, he thoughtfully covered the city's ever-changing culinary landscape like no other for *LA Weekly* and then the *Los Angeles Times,* and as a regular contributor to KCRW's program *Good Food* with Evan Kleiman, before he passed away in 2018. He placed the same value on the smallest of food stands and family-run eateries in strip malls as he would a celebrity chef-run restaurant, helping launch them into the national spotlight.

In addition to widening the city's palates, Gold holds significance for personal reasons. At a time when you'd find few outside the community dining at Filipino food establishments, Jonathan Gold sought out our cuisine and regularly covered it. He also gave me the opportunity in 2003 to contribute to *LA Weekly*'s annual "Best of L.A." issue, with entries on Philippines-based chains Jollibee in the "Best Fast-Food Breakfast" category and Max's Restaurant for "Best Halo-Halo," a Filipino shaved-ice dessert. In tribute to him, I recently visited some of his picks with our mutual friend, novelist Jervey Tervalon; they're now permanently on my go-to restaurant list, and I suggest you go, too.

Gold's favorite Thai restaurant in the city, and mine as well, is **Jitlada Restaurant** (5233 Sunset Blvd., Thai Town, 323/667-8909, http://jitladala.com), located in a strip mall in Thai Town. It's celebrated for its spicy Southern Thai food, and its two narrow dining rooms

morning glory salad at .litlada Restaurant

jambalaya and po'boy at The Little Jewel of New Orleans

Chichén Itzá's *cochinito pibil* torta

tacos and ceviche at Holbox

are always packed at night with patrons enjoying dishes such as lemongrass turmeric chicken soup and Crying Tiger grilled beef (featured on the Food Network's *The Best Thing I Ever Ate*), or the off-menu, hot-as-hell Jazz Burger by chef Jazz Singsanong. On the night we visited, we lucked out on a table near the entrance, auspiciously close to a framed photo of Gold. We savored every bite of the addictive morning glory salad (deep-fried greens with shrimp, cabbage, and onions), *pad woonsen* chicken (glass noodles, carrots, mushrooms), and *tom kha* tofu (soup with coconut milk). You can choose your spice level for each dish; if you're a spice aficionado and over 18—yes, there is an age minimum for this order—get the hottest item on the menu: Chef Tui's Spicy Dynamite Challenge, a stir-fry with your choice of meat.

The Little Jewel of New Orleans Grocery & Deli (207 Ord St., 213/620-0461, http://littlejewel.la), by chef-owner Marcus Christiana-Beniger and wife Eunah Kang, is located off a quiet street in Chinatown. Look for the green-and-white-striped awning outside. Gold's mom, Judith, was from northern Louisiana, and Tervalon's family from New Orleans, so the Little Jewel provided a taste of home, serving incredibly filling Creole food (the

▲ menu wall at The Little Jewel of New Orleans Grocery & Deli

sandwiches in particular are massive). The menu is creatively and colorfully chalked on the wall, and small tables and chairs are scattered across the turquoise-and-black checkerboard floor. A green picket fence—likely the only restaurant sporting one in L.A.!—separates the dining room from the small grocery. This counter-service spot draws people of all ages, from all walks of life, and jazz and Creole music plays on the speakers, making for a cool scene. Among the most popular menu items are the jambalaya and fried oyster po' boy. I was happily stuffed with my Louisiana fried catfish po' boy. Each table has Cajun seasoning Slap Ya Mama on it—be sure to use it!

In South L.A. is the **Mercado la Paloma** (3655 S. Grand Ave., www.mercadolapaloma. com), which has become a foodie destination in the Figueroa Corridor area. The complex is home to many international food stalls where you order at the counter and $20 goes a long way. Must-visits are the two Yucatán eateries by chef Gilberto Cetina Jr.: **Chichén Itzá** (C6, 213/741-1075, www.chichenitzarestaurant.com) and sister restaurant **Holbox** (C9, 213/986-9972, www.holboxla.com), which focuses on seafood. At Chichén Itzá, get the *cochinita pibil* (slow-roasted pork) torta with pickled onions and side of potato salad and tortilla chips; the dish tastes as good after reheating for a midnight snack as it does served fresh. The housemade habanero hot sauce here is non-negotiable; pour it on everything—it's my new alarm clock! At Holbox, try the ceviche *mixto,* with shrimp, octopus, local fish, and a dotted trail of avocado cream sauce around it—appropriate for "fine" white-tablecloth dining and, here, a mere $10. Also be sure to check out the specials board (on the day we visited, we got and downed the battered dogfish tacos). Should blood clams be on the menu, note Gold listed them in 2017 as an essential dish. If you're lucky, you may also catch one of the occasional community events that take place at the Mercado, from free live music and dance performances to art exhibits and speaking panels.

41 Take a Metro tour of Boyle Heights

Neighborhoods and City Streets • Art and Culture • Food and Drink • Shopping

Why Go: Hop along the L Line for a day of easy sightseeing, dining, and shopping in this bustling Mexican American neighborhood.

Where: Along E. 1st in Boyle Heights • Metro L Line (Gold) to Pico/Aliso, Mariachi Plaza, and Indiana

Timing: Metro L Line (Gold) light rail trains depart every 12-20 minutes (4am-12:30am daily). Make this a day-to-night adventure. An especially festive time to visit is during Día de los Muertos (Oct.-Nov. 2).

When the **Metro L Line (Gold)** (www.metro.net., one-way ride $1.75, day pass $7) opened its Eastside extension from Union Station to Boyle Heights and East L.A. in 2009, eager Angelenos packed trains to be among the first to ride it (my friend Pierpaolo was on the design team for two of the stations, so we were especially excited). It is important to acknowledge that each Metro rail addition forever changes the communities it runs through—residents who now have to live with the noise and rumble of passing trains, and people whose homes or businesses are demolished to make way for it. It also can bring welcomed new pedestrian traffic to businesses neighboring stations, and more efficient travel options and connections to neighborhoods across the city.

Spending a day hopping on and off the L Line in Boyle Heights is an easy way to experience some of the Mexican American community's treasured landmarks and hubs. First stop: Get out at the **Pico/Aliso Station** to visit **Self Help Graphics & Art** (1300 E. 1st St., 323/881-6444, www.selfhelpgraphics.com), in the building directly across from the station's platform. It was founded in 1973 to provide Chicano/a and Latinx artists a place to creatively express their history and heritage through art, particularly printmaking. It also programs public art exhibits, events, and workshops focused on media such as screenprinting, ceramics, and murals. On the building's exterior you can admire the ***Una Trenza*** mural, created by 15 local artists, then head inside to see what's happening that day.

1: Espacio 1839 **2:** Mariachi Plaza Station entrance **3:** La Sagrada Familia booth at El Mercadito **4:** Self Help Graphics & Art building near the Pico/Aliso Station

Next stop: **Mariachi Plaza Station,** one stop east on the L Line. At concourse level is Sonia Romera's vibrant Chicanx mural ***Hecho a Mano,*** developed with the local community (including Self Help) to highlight local residents past and present, including Mexican, Japanese, and Jewish Americans. Take the stairs up to plaza level to view ***El Niño Perdido*** ("the lost child") by Boyle Heights artist Alejandro de La Loza, a poignant bronze sculpture of a woman with her arms outstretched holding a baby, inspired by the Mexican song of the same name about a mother and child reuniting.

Mariachi Plaza (1st St. and Boyle Ave.) is so named because mariachi groups have congregated here since the 1930s, singing to passersby and hanging out hoping to be hired for an event. The Mexico state of Jalisco, considered the birthplace of mariachi, donated the plaza's stone bandstand, and Jalisco artisans created and gifted to the city the wrought-iron benches surrounding it. Also on the plaza is a sculpture honoring the pioneering Mexican mariachi singer Lucha Reyes. Musicians continue to socialize and perform in the plaza, in the bandstand and on its steps, with larger performances held on the stage behind the Metro

▲ Mariachi Plaza

station's exit. For a potential serenade and Mexican fare, visit longtime plaza fixture **Santa Cecilia** (1707 Mariachi Plaza, 323/980-0716), order a combo platter, and feast outside.

Catty-corner from the plaza is tailor Jorge Tello's **La Casa Del Mariachi** (1836 E. 1st St., 323/262-5243, http://lacasadelmariachi.shop), which mariachi turn to for master handiwork. Shop the selection of embroidered shirts and accessories. Across the street is **Espacio 1839** (1839 E. 1st. St., 323/265-3730, www.espacio1839.com), which exhibits works by local artists as well as stocks gift items, apparel, and accessories (the earring line is incredible) by Chicano/a and Mexican makers and artisans. There is whimsy, humor, and beauty in the shop's inventory, like its T-shirts expressing Mexican and Boyle Heights pride ("Selena Is My Homegirl" and "Brown Like the Earth") and social justice messages ("Read and Decolonize"). Espacio 1839 also has a built-in studio, **Radio Espacio,** where community members can broadcast from or record podcasts, free of charge.

Final Metro stop: **Indiana Station,** two stops southeast from Mariachi Plaza. It's located right near a major hub, the always busy **El Mercadito** (3425 E. 1st St.). Open since 1968, today it is where the Mexican community comes to shop, dine, and catch up with friends. The three-story indoor marketplace hosts vendors selling everything from groceries and clay cooking pots to rosaries and *huaraches* (Mexican weaved sandals). Browse vendors like **La Sagrada Familia** (stalls #14 and 49), filled with statues of religious figures and Mexican folk heroes, and **Artesan La Ortega** (stall #16 and 29) for pottery and sculptures. Sit-down cateries include the **Mariachi Restaurant** (323/268-3451), where you can catch live music at night, and **El Gallito Restaurant** (323/266-0127). You can also pick up fruit drinks and snacks from one of the many food stalls; I love the Tostiesquites (chips topped with Mexican corn, chili powder, sour cream, and lime) from **Las Palmitas** (stall #8). Bring cash.

Connect with . . .

21 Celebrate life and death during Día de los Muertos

36 Get creative with local artisans

42 Catch rising SoCal stars at the Vincent Price Art Museum

Art and Culture • For All Ages

Why Go: Highlighting the work of local Latinx artists, this community college-based museum has helped launch many into the national spotlight.

Where: East Los Angeles College, 1301 Avenida Cesar Chavez, Monterey Park • 323/265-8831 • http://vincentpriceartmuseum.org • free admission • Metro bus 70 to East LA College or Metro bus 106 to ELAC Transit Center

Timing: Allow a couple of hours to take in all of the exhibits. Check the calendar for art openings in spring and fall and free workshops.

The suburb city of Monterey Park in the San Gabriel Valley is not generally considered among the top destinations to experience art. But some of my favorite exhibits in recent years have been here—at **East Los Angeles College (ELAC),** home to the **Vincent Price Art Museum (VPAM).** You might be wondering, what does Vincent Price have to do with fine art? The actor, with his trademark thin mustache, is more commonly associated with the many horror movies in which he appeared, including *The Raven* (1963) and *The Masque of the Red Death* (1964), so much so that Tim Burton paid him homage with a small but significant part in *Edward Scissorhands* (1990). But he studied art history before acting and was also an art collector. After visiting ELAC on various occasions in the early 1950s, he and his wife, Mary Grant, noticed the lack of arts education and access to art objects on campus and wanted to address this; in 1957, they donated 90 artworks, ranging from Mesoamerican artifacts to African artwork, to ELAC's art gallery, which was subsequently renamed in their honor. Over time, the Prices would go on to donate a total of around 2,000 works.

Located in a tall building with geometrically shaped cutout windows that scream 21st century, the museum stands out in an area dominated by chain stores and restaurants and is a source of neighborhood pride. ELAC is the first community college to house a teaching art collection—it offers a museum studies program, and students who work at VPAM are trained to work in the museum field—and among the few U.S. community colleges to have a major art

 Vincent Price Art Museum

lobby of the Vincent Price Art Museum

Form and Function in the Ancient Americas exhibit

collection. VPAM's 40,000 square feet spans three floors, with seven galleries—two are set aside for student learning labs—and a multimedia lecture hall.

Free for all to enter, it has more than 9,000 pieces in its collection spanning various media, time periods, and countries, and is prized for its ancient artworks and textiles from Central and South America. Items from the permanent collection are on display in the museum's ongoing ***Form and Function in the Ancient Americas*** exhibit. Here you'll find items including pre-Columbian artworks, textiles, and ceramics from Peru and Mexico, notably earthenware originating from West Mexico.

VPAM also hosts temporary **special exhibits** that generally focus on the work of contemporary artists, with one gallery dedicated to multimedia shows, such as immersive video installations. In recent years, VPAM has received attention for showcasing work by local artists—in particular those who reflect the school's diverse student body and surrounding community, which is home to large populations of Hispanic/Latino and Asian Americans. Many of these artists—such as the late Chicana photographer Laura Aguilar and mixed-me-

▲ photographer George Rodriguez with his N.W.A. portrait at his 2019 solo retrospective

Where to Eat in Monterey Park

Monterey Park is known as a destination for authentic Asian food. Before or after you visit VPAM, try a breakfast of sweet and savory buns with freshly made hot soy milk at **Huge Tree Pastry** (423 N. Atlantic Blvd., 626/458-8689), go for *xiao long bao* (soup dumplings) at **Mama Lu's Dumpling House** (501 W. Garvey Ave., 626/282-2256, http://mamaludumpling.com), or pick from a variety of noodles—choose your size, spice level, and order dry or in soup!—at **Noodle Art** (117 N. Lincoln Ave., 626/999-3099, www.noodleartusa.com).

dia and neon artist Patrick Martinez went on to receive national recognition. The vision of VPAM director Steven Wong, previously a curator at the Chinese American Museum and Los Angeles Municipal Art Gallery, is to maintain a focus on Latinx artists while also looking broadly at intersections with Asian American and Pacific Islander communities, addressing issues that are relevant to all. These special exhibits often focus minutely on important aspects of L.A. culture and identity that tend to be underexplored in large museum settings.

Two recent shows that I had the pleasure of reporting on captured the art and activist communities of L.A. in ways I had not seen before. The 2018 exhibit *Regeneración: Three Generations of Revolutionary Ideology,* curated by then-VPAM director Pilar Tompkins Rivas, told the resistance stories of Chicana and Mexican women—such as artists and activists Aida Salazar and Patricia Valencia—spanning the 1900s to 1990s, as revealed through personal correspondence, newspaper clippings, and archival videos. The 2019 solo retrospective *George Rodriguez: Double Vision,* curated by Josh Kun, covered more than 40 years of the photographer's work. Among the photos was one of the most published of Cesar Chavez. Other notable photos ranged from a wall-sized image of the 1970 Chicano Moratorium march in Boyle Heights, when thousands of Mexican Americans marched in protest against the Vietnam War, to a 1990 photo shoot with Compton rap legends N.W.A. What do the Chicano Moratorium and N.W.A. have in common besides who photographed them? That's the kind of dialogue a VPAM exhibit inspires.

43 Picnic and park-hop in seaside San Pedro

Get Outside • Get Out of Town• For All Ages

Why Go: Find open green spaces with coastal views and tide pool access right in the city.

Where: About 25 miles south of Downtown via I-110 • Metro bus 246 to Shepard/Gaffey

Timing: It takes 30 minutes to drive to the San Pedro neighborhood from Downtown. Plan on an all-day adventure and a couple of easy miles of meandering. It gets windy by the water, so bring a blanket or jacket and, perhaps, a kite.

I have an enduring love for the South Bay, especially the coastal neighborhood of San Pedro. I lived nearby for a few years as a child, and regularly visit my *titas* (aunts) in neighboring Harbor City. Two generations of my family, including my *lola* (grandmother), are buried in the area. I have vivid childhood memories of weekends spent in San Pedro, eating fresh seafood at the charming, now-demolished Ports O' Call Village on the waterfront and catching the ferry to Catalina Island. As an adult, my experiences here have ranged from touring artist studios to attending a house party at Marymount California University. These days, I can't direct you to any rowdy college gatherings in the area, but I can suggest a satisfying, laid-back excursion exploring the parks (310/548-7705, www.laparks.org) lining the San Pedro cliffs.

Many people are surprised that San Pedro is actually part of Los Angeles—the southernmost part, in fact. The neighborhood is a straight shot south down the 110 freeway from Downtown, and you'll know you're there when you see its most prominent landmark—the green **Vincent Thomas Bridge,** a pile-supported suspension bridge also known as "San Pedro's Golden Gate"—along with the endless stacks of colorful shipping containers (where many Hollywood action scenes have been shot) and towering cranes denoting the Port of Los Angeles. Not everyone finds this industrial coastline a thing of beauty, but stay with me. Exit at North Gaffey Street, one of San Pedro's main drags, and continue on toward the ocean. The

Point Fermin Lighthouse

Korean Friendship Bell in Angels Gate Park

view from Point Fermin Park

majority of storefronts and buildings along the street seem trapped in the 1970s and '80s, but with new, modern waterfront developments in the works, we'll see what emerges.

Along the way to the water, pick up some takeout for a seaside picnic. Consider calling in an order ahead of time to the busy **Sandwich Saloon** (813 S. Gaffey St., 310/548-5322, www.sandwichsaloondeli.com) or beloved diner **Omelette & Waffle Shop** (1103 S. Gaffey St., 310/831-3277), within a few blocks of each other. Down the street, take note of Mexican bar and grill **Puesta Del Sol** (1622 S. Gaffey St., 310/833-9765, http://puestadelsolsp.com) as a possible dinner option on the way home.

At the end of Gaffey Street is your first destination: the 37-acre **Point Fermin Park** (807 W. Paseo Del Mar), located at the tip of the San Pedro peninsula, set on the cliffs above the Pacific. You can park your car for the day here for free, and everything on this itinerary is easily walkable from the park. Cross the grassy field to walk the pathway along the bluff's edge and take in expansive views of the coastline. Try to snag one of the park's picnic pavilions overlooking the ocean, or plant yourself in the shade of one of the massive palm trees, and enjoy your provisions. After, as you wander the park, stay on the paved pathways and marked trails for your safety.

Near the park's center is an open-air amphitheater that hosts free cultural events such as **Shakespeare by the Sea** (310/213-7596, www.shakespearebythesea.org, Fri.-Sun. summer) and **Music by the Sea** (Sun. July-Aug.). Just beyond it is the cream Stick-style, green-shuttered **Point Fermin Lighthouse** (310/241-0684, http://pointferminlighthouse.org, donation suggested), constructed in 1874. You can learn about its fascinating history and unique architecture on a tour.

From the lighthouse, take the cliffside sidewalk and head west out of the park and along Paseo Del Mar for a little more than a half mile to **Wilders Addition Park** (607 W. Paseo Del Mar). Here you'll find two trails to the rocky beach below, where you can marvel at the marinelife in the tide pools: crabs, sea urchins, California sea hares, anemones. If you're lucky, you might also see a snowy egret. The tide can be moody at times, so be careful along the rocks.

Head back east on Paseo del Mar, then cross the street, going inland, to visit with locals (and their dogs) at **Joan Milke Flores Park** (834 Paseo Del Mar), from which you can

What's with the Photographers?

As you walk along Paseo Del Mar, you may notice many not-so-casual photographers—with mega-zoom lenses and tripods set up—hanging out in groups along the guardrails, some in camouflage attire. If they don't flash a smile your way or engage you in friendly conversation, it's because they have one goal in mind: to photograph **peregrine falcons,** the world's fastest animals, in action; the birds are often found around the coastal bluffs here. During spring, the falcons' mating season, you'll see them flying overhead and diving for prey at incredible speeds, along with upward of 70 photographers. Other birds you may spot in the vicinity include Cooper's hawks, western gulls, and brown pelicans.

hike up the hill to **Angels Gate Park** (3601 S. Gaffey St.), where you may see kite flyers (including, maybe, the regular who expertly flies his kite while lying down). Don't miss out on the chance to join them and fly your own if the weather's right; it's a San Pedro pastime. A must-see at Angels Gate is the ornately crafted bronze **Korean Friendship Bell,** housed in a magnificently decorated pavilion. Gifted by the people of South Korea in 1976 to the United States as a sign of friendship and to commemorate veterans of the Korean War, it was installed in Los Angeles because it's home to the largest Korean American population in the country. Angels Gate is a stunning spot to see the sunset over the ocean, and worth lingering at afterward to see the pavilion light up at night.

44 Wander the tide pools at Abalone Cove Beach

Get Out of Town • Get Outside • For All Ages

Why Go: It's a challenge and a joy to explore the marinelife and magnificent rock formations on this stretch of coast.

Where: 5970 Palos Verdes Dr. S., Rancho Palos Verdes • 310/544-5366 • www.rpv-ca.gov • Metro bus 344 to Palos Verdes/Sea Cove or Palos Verdes Peninsula Transit Authority Gold or Orange Lines to Palos Verdes Dr. S./Wayfarers Chapel

Timing: Come at low tide; check the National Oceanic and Atmospheric Administration site (https://tidesandcurrents.noaa.gov) for a tide report. Spend a half or whole day here.

Rancho Palos Verdes, just 30 miles south of Downtown L.A. and perched damn prettily on the **Palos Verdes Peninsula** atop coastal bluffs, is a nearby escape from which you can take scenic trails down to the beach. My family is a fan of Abalone Cove Beach in particular, which has tide pools full of colorful sealife, striking rock formations, and a sandy beach.

Getting to the beach along our preferred route requires traversing some tricky (but fun!) terrain that's manageable for children and adults—so long as you're wearing the right shoes! When you think "beach," you probably think flip-flops will do, but for Abalone Cove, it's wise to wear shoes with good traction (better yet, waterproof ones). This outing is just over a half mile one-way from the parking lot, but an adventurous one that should not be rushed, as you will cross some rocky sections.

Park at **Abalone Cove Shoreline Park** and take in the expanse of gleaming Pacific from the wide-open space. There's plenty of space to spread out, though few trees, so bring a hat on sunnier days. If you packed a picnic, you'll want to eat it at the park, which has picnic tables, grassy areas, public restrooms, and trash cans. Plus—trust me—you won't want to be burdened by any extra weight on your way to the beach.

When you're ready, walk to the oceanfront fence line, which puts you on the **Via de Campo Trail.** Follow it east for a few minutes until you reach the opening in the fence; walk

▲ Abalone Cove Beach

▲ enjoying the rock formations at low tide

through it and you'll soon find yourself on the **Abalone Cove Trail,** marked with signage. Descending the narrow trail takes just five minutes, but you'll want to pause to take a picture during spring and summer, when black mustard flowers bloom on both sides of the trail, engulfing hikers in a lovely way.

The path ends at the rocky beach. From here you'll walk east across hundreds of rocks of varying sizes to reach the sand; tread carefully, though most are quite stable from years of people walking over them. (If you want to skip the rocks, you can also make your way via a series of waterfront trails that connect to Abalone Cove Trail.) Then follow the beach to the coastal bluff to enjoy tide pools full of marinelife—such as sea hares, mollusks, and urchins—amid magnificent cascading layers of rock that feel otherworldly. I have faint memories of taking a field trip here when I was in elementary school, and wonder if I uttered the same excited "oohs" and "aahhs" each time I came across a crab or sea anemone as my young daughter does when we visit.

From the tide pool area, you can also look west toward the far hills and see a cross atop a

along the Abalone Cove Trail

The Cliffside Chapel of Glass

While you can see it from afar, it's even more remarkable up close: Lloyd Wright's 1951 masterpiece, the **Wayfarers Chapel** (5755 Palos Verdes Dr. S., 310/377-1650, www. wayfarerschapel.org), overlooks the Pacific Ocean and is just a 15-minute walk from Abalone Cove Shoreline Park. Surrounded by redwoods, the chapel is one of Southern California's most in-demand wedding venues due to its dreamlike environs (chances are high you'll catch a wedding in progress during your visit). Light floods through the predominantly glass structure in dramatic, heavenly fashion. Walk the beautifully land-scaped grounds, meditate at the reflection pool, and stop by the visitors center and gift shop.

tower, surrounded by trees. That's the site of the Wayfarers Chapel, designed by Frank Lloyd Wright's son, Lloyd Wright.

On the beach, draw your names in the sand, study the seaweed and shells that've washed up, or take a dip in the water, where you may encounter surfers enjoying the waves. You may be tempted to take a souvenir home, but Abalone Cove is part of a protected ecological reserve, so enjoy the area and its many natural wonders, but don't disturb or take home any marinelife or rocks. Note that no dogs are allowed on the beach.

After your day's adventure, if you're ready for a meal before traveling back to the city, head to the **Terranea Resort** (100 Terranea Way, 855/938-4047, www.terranea.com). The posh resort is only a five-minute drive west of the beach, with al fresco dining options ranging in level of luxury and price. Just come as you are; there are casual options. Our family, ranging from elementary-school kids to septuagenarians, has enjoyed the **Lobby Bar & Terrace** for its ocean views and laidback ambience.

45 Play in the snow and sand on the same day

Get Outside • Get Out of Town • For All Ages

Why Go: Take advantage of being in a city where you have easy access to both the ocean and the mountains.

Where: Angeles National Forest and Santa Monica State Beach

Timing: Plan this day-long adventure between mid-November and early February. Arrive in the mountains by 9am before parking lots get packed, and leave for the coastline after lunch to hit the sand well before sunset.

Los Angeles is known for its miles of stunning coastline. But it's also close to the San Gabriel Mountains in the Angeles National Forest, which, during late fall and winter, are snow covered. For a fun day out, enjoy L.A.'s proximity to both summery and wintry landscapes.

Start your day off in the snow and then end it back in the city for sand. Dress and pack for both terrains and temperatures (including snow chains, just in case, and a sled or saucer), and pack a picnic lunch. From Downtown, the 2 (also called the Glendale Freeway) becomes the Angeles Crest Highway and takes you northeast into Angeles National Forest. You can turn off at various points along the highway to play in the snow, but I suggest parking at one of the picnic areas for open spaces and restrooms. Purchase a Forest Adventure Pass ($5 day-use fee, $30 annual pass), which is required at most parking lots in Angeles National Forest; you can pick one up at stores such as REI and Big 5 as well as the Shell station in La Cañada Flintridge (4530 Angeles Crest Hwy.), which is on the way. Before heading out, check for road closures with **Angeles National Forest** (747/322-6574, www.fs.usda.gov) or **CalTrans** (800/427-7623, http://roads.dot.ca.gov).

Just 28 miles northeast of Downtown is one of Angeles National Forest's most popular snow-play spots, the **Red Box Picnic Area** (Angeles Crest Hwy. and Mt. Wilson Red Box Rd.), at an elevation of 4,640 feet. The winding Mount Wilson Red Box Road that runs next to it is closed to vehicles when it snows—and steep enough to sled on. Expect to see fami-

1: into Angeles National Forest 2: snow-capped San Gabriel Mountains 3: Santa Monica State Beach 4: wading in the water at Santa Monica State Beach

lies building snowpeople and having snowball fights. One of the picnic area's parking lots puts you right at the doorstep of the **Haramokngna American Indian Cultural Center** (626/449-8975, http://haramokngna.org, free), a small museum that's worth visiting while you're here. It highlights the region's tribes as well as offers cool programs on subjects such as foraging, and the volunteers can tell you a lot about the history of the land and offer tips on where to play or hike in the area any time of year. During winter months, the center also sells gloves and beanies if you forgot yours at home.

If you want to go deeper into the forest, continue another 10 miles east on Angeles Crest Highway for another favorite snow-play destination, **Charlton Flats Picnic Area** (Forest Service Rd. 3N16), at an elevation of 5,400 feet and home to some of the longest pinecones in the world—averaging a foot long—thanks to the sugar pines here. You won't have to venture far to find friendly flat areas amid the trees where you can make snow angels or snowshoe. For newcomers, forest rangers suggest starting at the area's first upper parking lot (take a

Santa Monica State Beach at sunset

right when you reach a fork in the road upon first entering). At the south end of it, a short wooden bridge leads to picnic tables and various trails.

After you've had your fill of snow, it's time to hit the sand. **Santa Monica State Beach** (310/458-8300, www.smgov.net) is a 55-mile drive southwest of Charlton Flats via the 2, the 10, and the Pacific Coast Highway. If traffic cooperates, you can drive between these snow and sand destinations within 1.5 hours. My preferred stretch of sand is near the **Annenberg Community Beach House** (415 Pacific Coast Hwy., 310/458-4904, www. annenbergbeachhouse.com, winter parking $3 per hour or $8 per day), a public beach house that was originally the private estate of actress Marion Davies. It's about a mile and half away from the touristy but lovable Santa Monica Pier—which means it's much less crowded—and is especially great for families with young kids because of its close proximity to desirable amenities, including a kids' playground, convenient outdoor showers, super-clean bathrooms, and a lifeguard tower. A plus is the paved path from the playground that runs to just near the water's edge if you want to avoid trekking across the sand. Pack a soccer ball or volleyball to make use of the public soccer nets and volleyball courts here! Nearby is the **Back on the Beach Café** (445 Pacific Coast Hwy., 310/393-8282, www.backonthebeachcafe.com), where you can you grab a meal to enjoy outside while burying your feet in the sand. You can also rent sand chairs and umbrellas here, then find a spot on the wide expanse of beach stretching in both directions. The water will be chilly at this time of year, but that doesn't keep my family from playing in the ocean, or other people from bodyboarding. Stay to watch the sun set to end your day with a sweet SoCal embrace.

Call it a day or, for a bookending wintry bonus, head to **Ice at Santa Monica** (1324 5th St., 310/260-1199, http://iceatsantamonica.com, mid-Nov.-early Feb.), where you can enjoy ice-skating on an 8,000-square-foot rink. It's a pretty 30-minute walk on the paved **Ocean Front Walk** from the Annenberg Community Beach House. At night it's especially festive, with string lights encircling the rink and multicolored lanterns overhead.

46 Pick fresh produce from SoCal farms

Get Out of Town • Food and Drink • For All Ages • Get Outside

Why Go: These destination-worthy farms offer bountiful fruits and veggies, wagon rides, and special events.

Where: Underwood Family Farms (50 miles northwest of L.A.) and Tanaka Farms (45 miles southeast of L.A.)

Timing: Both farms are open year-round and are an hour away (in opposite directions) from L.A. Check their websites to see what's in season. Fall—when there are pumpkin patches and special events—is the busiest time.

If you're a kid in Los Angeles, at some point either your school or your parent is going to take you to a farm. L.A. has many community gardens and urban farms, providing valuable opportunities for people to grow their own food or learn about the process, but for an amusement-park kind of experience that your kids won't forget, leave the city limits. Two farms dominate Angelenos' itineraries, with numerous offerings and activities and landscapes that make a lovely backdrop for dates or family and friend outings.

I had never heard of Ventura County's **Underwood Family Farms** (3370 Sunset Valley Rd., Moorpark, 805/529-3690, www.underwoodfamilyfarms.com, standard admission $6-8 adults, free for children 2 and under, additional fees for some activities), even when I lived in the area as a teenager, but so ingrained is it in the minds of every young kid's parent in L.A. that everyone just refers to it as "Underwood." I understood after our first visit; it is the ultimate kid playground. Underwood's attractions include multiple recreation areas (slides, trike trail, swings), wagon rides, and an animal center, in addition to its produce market and pick-your-own experiences—for which you can opt to take a wagon ride or grab a pull wagon and walk to the fields yourself. We've enjoyed picking the farm's radishes, fennel, and strawberries in the past. Underwood's biggest event is its **Fall Harvest Festival** (late Sept.-Oct., admission $16-22), when the farm transforms into a party scene best described as "Fallapalooza" for kids. You can wander around select areas blanketed with pumpkins and

1: picking flowers at Tanaka Farms' Hana Field
2: horse-drawn wagon ride at Underwood
Family Farms **3:** a chicken at Tanaka Farms
4: a tractor-pulled ride at Underwood

fresh corn at Tanaka Farms

daisies at Hana Field

a trail for trikes at Underwood Family Farms

pick some to take home, and there are multiple perfect pumpkin patch photo ops. Lines will be longer for all the attractions, but it's something to experience at least once!

In Orange County, **Tanaka Farms** (5380 3/4 University Dr., Irvine, 949/653-2100, www.tanakafarms.com, prices vary for tours and special events) grows more than 60 types of fruits and vegetables that are harvested daily. The farm is an example of the valuable role and long history of Japanese Americans in California agriculture; established in 1940, it has been proudly run by the Tanakas for four generations. The grounds include a large tented market stand and gift shop where you can purchase their produce as well as specialty food items, such as honey and jam made locally. There are also themed farm tours such as the **Farm to Table Cookout Tours,** a two to three hour guided walking and picking tour, during which visitors select vegetables from the fields (such as kale, corn, carrots, and eggplant) to bring home, and then proceed to the farm's cookout area for a freshly prepared lunch of grilled veggies, salad, and fruit. Special events include the **pumpkin patch and corn maze** (Oct.) and the twinkling **Hikari: Festival of Lights** (Dec.), when you can tour the farm—lit with colorful lanterns and more than a million lights—by wagon. There are also fruit-focused, tractor-pulled wagon tour experiences: **Strawberry Tours** (Mar.-June) and, our pick, **Melon Tours** (July-Aug.), during which my family got to enjoy tastings of different types of watermelons (yellow and red, with and without seeds) and other produce as well as pick some of our own. When I asked my daughter what she liked most about our visit, she said, "All the eating!"

For a bonus treat on your way to or from Tanaka Farms, stop by **Hana Field** (427 Anton Blvd., Costa Mesa, admission $5, spring only), also operated by Tanaka Farms and just seven miles west, a truly magical place (marriage proposals have been known to take place on the grounds). Here you can wander rows of flowers and herbs—right next to freeway overpasses. But that's part of its beauty. *Hana* means "flower" in Japanese, and the main attraction here are the towering sunflowers, but there are also zinnias, snapdragons, and more. Pay an extra $20 for a cup to fill with the flowers of your choice.

47 Enjoy nearby nature and small-town charm in Ojai

Get Out of Town • Get Outside

Why Go: This century-old city nestled in the Ojai Valley offers easy access to surrounding green spaces.

Where: 85 miles northwest of L.A. via U.S. 101 and Highway 33

Timing: It's a two-hour drive to Ojai from L.A., so plan on at least a full day if not the whole weekend. Summer can be hot in the valley, so consider coming outside the season.

For thousands of years, the Chumash Indians lived in the Ojai Valley, between the Topatopa Mountains and Sulphur Mountain. The name "Ojai" is derived from the Ventureño Chumash word *'awha'y,* whose exact meaning is disputed but translates as either "nest" or "moon." This magical landscape and the riches it offers continue to be prized today; there's a long history of philosophers, spiritual thinkers, and artists residing in the valley. While it's easy to get around in a car, part of the allure of Ojai is that its green spaces and trails are so walkable from the town center.

The city of Ojai is just four square miles and has a picturesque small-town feel, in no small part thanks to its Spanish-style architecture as well as a ban on large chains to protect its mom-and-pop stores. Start your day at one of them, busy **Bonnie Lu's** (328 E. Ojai Ave., 805/646-0207, www.bonnieluscafe.com). Pick up a sandwich to go (there will be lots of places to picnic on the day's adventure) or dine in if you're feeling leisurely. The cute eatery is in the middle of town along the main drag of **Ojai Avenue,** which you'll want to stroll at some point to peruse more restaurants, shops, and a smattering of wine-tasting rooms and breweries.

Cross the street and walk west half a block to enter the town's lovely **Libbey Park** (205 E. Ojai Ave.) through one of its white archways. Meander south through the park along the paved path past the tennis courts to find **Libbey Bowl** (866/654-5006, http://libbeybowl.

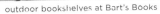
outdoor bookshelves at Bart's Books

Ojai Meadows Preserve

en route to the Valley View Preserve

org), an outdoor venue encircled by trees where concerts are held in summer and early fall. Notice the sycamore tree to the right of the bowl; it's more than two centuries old. Local lore suggests the Chumash bent it as a sapling to form an arch to indicate a camping spot or the start of a trail, and was later viewed as a Peace Tree—where no battles were to be had—or a Marriage Tree, for a couple to walk under for the Great Spirit to unite them.

Directly behind the bowl, hop onto the flat **Ojai Valley Trail,** a greenway for pedestrians and bicyclists. Head west on it for about a mile to the small **Rotary Community Park** (Ojai Valley Trail at Hwy. 33), pausing to read uplifting quotes by notable residents and historical figures engraved in stone slabs. From here, depart from the Ojai Valley Trail to follow Highway 33 west for a half mile, just past Nordhoff High School, to reach **Ojai Meadows Preserve** (1601 Maricopa Hwy./Hwy. 33, http://ovlc.org). Here you can walk the level 0.6-mile **Meadows Preserve Loop.** The first part runs alongside the school's sports field, but then you're completely immersed in the natural landscape, including wetlands and dramatic mountain backdrops. You might spot California quails, western scrub-jays and kingbirds, and black and Say's phoebes, or maybe a tree frog, spotted skunk (hopefully, not startling it), or western brush rabbit.

From here, walk back to town, or save some energy for later and pay the small fee to catch the **Ojai Trolley** (http://ojaitrolley.com) at the Pirie Road intersection in front of the high school. Get off at the Ojai/Canada stop and walk a block north to **Bart's Books** (302 W. Matilija St., 805/646-3755, http://bartsbooksojai.com), opened in 1964 and alone worth the drive to Ojai. Based in the former residence of the original owner, Richard "Bart" Bartinsdale, the bookstore offers a wonderful maze of literature to get lost in (mostly gently used books) and is largely open-air, with seating areas around a patio and in front of stacks. But you can also go inside to the study, kitchen, and other rooms, where you'll find shelves, counters, and corners packed with books. This is a great place to stop in for rare and first editions.

When you're feeling hungry, head to **Ojai Rôtie** (469 E. Ojai Ave, 805/798-9227, www.ojairotie.com) for picnic-friendly French Lebanese fare, including rotisserie chicken, skewers, charred eggplant, and house-made organic bread you'll want to stock up on. Even better, it has a spacious outdoor patio with picnic tables and trees for shade.

After recharging, head north via Signal Street until it turns into Shelf Road. The paved road ends at the **Valley View Preserve** (http://ovlc.org), a short drive or 30-minute walk from the restaurant. You'll see a gate marking the start of the **Shelf Road Trail,** which brings you, after a five-minute walk, to an informational bulletin board showing the preserve's trail system. Choose your adventure. **Fox Canyon Trail** zigzags 800 feet up the canyon for just over a mile, and there's also the steep 0.75-mile **Luci's Trail,** both of which connect to other trails at their ends. Or remain on Shelf Road Trail and walk to its end about two miles east.

If you're ready to call it a day, head south out of town and be sure to pull off the 101 at any exit once you hit the coastline to treat your feet to some sand and a little ocean soak at Ventura Beach before the car ride back. Or, if you're staying to catch one of Ojai's legendary pink sunsets and spend the night, options include the rustic **Ojai Rancho Inn** (615 W. Ojai Ave., 805/646-1434, www.ojairanchoinn.com) and the luxurious **Ojai Valley Inn** (905 Country Club Rd., 855/697-8780, www.ojaivalleyinn.com).

48 Get away to Santa Barbara

Get Out of Town • Food and Drink • Shopping

Why Go: Santa Barbara and the nearby village of Montecito offer diversions for every taste under the sun along a stretch of beautiful coastline.

Where: 95 miles northwest of L.A. via U.S. 101 • Amtrak *Pacific Surfliner* or *Coast Starlight* to Santa Barbara

Timing: By car, it takes about 2 hours to drive up the coast from L.A.; by train it takes 2.5 hours. A weekend is recommended.

I spent a significant chunk of my teenage years driving north along the scenic stretch of the 101 freeway that hugs the coastline on the way to Santa Barbara. Many days and nights I lingered in town, shopping at thrift stores and hanging out at cafés. It always felt like I was on holiday. Decades later, Santa Barbara—with its pretty, lively downtown featuring Mediterranean and Spanish Colonial Revival-style architecture sandwiched between the sea and the Santa Ynez Mountains—is still one of the best getaways for Angelenos.

Start your trip with a stroll downtown along the pretty, palm-lined main drag, **State Street,** a wide boulevard with loads of retail stores, bars, and restaurants. Those with a sweet tooth will enjoy the Santa Barbara-born ice cream chain **McConnell's** (728 State St., 805/324-4402, http://mcconnells.com), founded in 1949. Order an ice cream sandwich with freshly made cookies; I recommend the toasted coconut almond chip or pistachio amaretto. A few blocks up, **Lilac Pâtisserie** (1017 State St., 805/845-7400, http://lilacpatisserie.com) offers breakfast, lunch, and tasty gluten-free desserts (try the chocolate sea salt caramel cake). Another couple of blocks up, right off State, is the **Santa Barbara Public Market** (38 W. Victoria St., 805/770-7702, www.sbpublicmarket.com), where you can sample fare from local chefs, including small plates from friendly chef Ramon Velazquez of Mexican eatery **Corazon Cocina** (Unit 122, http://corazoncocinasb.com). He also has a background

State Street

Santa Barbara

as a sushi chef, reflected in his colorful Sal De Mar dish, which features seasonal sashimi, watermelon, and pomegranate.

Also just off State nearby is the **Santa Barbara Courthouse and Sunken Gardens** (1100 Anacapa St., 805/962-6464, http://sbcourthouse.org), a Spanish-Moorish complex completed in 1929. With its grand archways and clock tower—open to the public for a 360-degree view of the city—and surrounding lawns, including a large semi-sunken one (great for picnics!), it's the rare courthouse where people choose to get married not solely for its functionality but for its picturesque setting. The gardens also host free movies and live performances in summer; check the community calendar (www.sbac.ca.gov).

For more shopping, dining, and drinking, head to the **Funk Zone** (between State St. and Garden St. and Montecito St. and Cabrillo Blvd., www.funkzone.net), a district just off State. It's especially known for its numerous tasting rooms for wine, spirits, and craft beer made locally, including the **Santa Barbara Wine Collective** (131 Anacapa St. #C, 805/456-2700, www.santabarbarawinecollective.com), **Culter's Artisan Distillery** (17 Anacapa St. #D, 805/680-4009, http://cutlersartisan.com), and **Rincon Brewery** (205 Santa Barbara St., Ste. 1B, 805/869-6627, www.rinconbrewery.com).

From the Funk Zone it's a short walk to the city's waterfront. You'll understand why Santa Barbara has been called the American Riviera when you take in the ocean views and fresh air while you dig your feet into the sand or take a dip at **West Beach** (along W. Cabrillo Blvd.). Then play tourist and venture to the adjacent **Stearns Wharf** (http://stearnswharf.org); the nearly 2,000-foot pier (among the longest in California) was built in 1872. I recommend timing your walk to the pier's end to catch the sun setting into the Pacific. On the way, browse Santa Barbara merch at **Old Wharf Trading Company** (217 Stearns Wharf #A) or get your palm read by **Madame Rosinka** (221 Stearns Wharf #B). From the pier, you can also hop on a boat with **Celebration Cruises** (237 Stearns Wharf) for views of the city from the water.

If you're staying overnight, **Hotel Indigo** (121 State St., 805/966-6586, www.ihg.com/hotelindigo) puts you in close proximity to the city's action.

About five miles east of Santa Barbara is the village of **Montecito,** where you could easily spend a day. Stunning sunset and Channel Islands views can be had at **Butterfly Beach**

(1260 Channel Dr.). Many celebrities live in this wealthy enclave, and while they won't be inviting you for a visit, you can tour historic residences such as the **Ganna Walska Lotusland** (Cold Spring Rd., 805/869-9990, www.lotusland.org), which the Polish opera singer turned into a botanical wonderland featuring more than 3,500 plant species. Or visit the national historic landmark **Casa del Herrero** (1387 E. Valley Rd., 805/565-5653, www.casadelherrero.com), built in the 1920s for inventor George Fox Steedman and his wife, Carrie. Right down the street from the latter is the clapboard cottage store **William Laman Furniture.Garden.Antiques** (1946 E. Valley Rd., 805/969-2840, http://williamlaman.com), which offers a distinct mix of home furnishings and gifts, from affordable and chic bamboo flower holders to a break-the-bank French lotus table. Not to be missed is a visit to the 1893 **San Ysidro Ranch** (900 San Ysidro Ln., 805/368 6788, www.sanysidroranch.com), a resort of cottages tucked away in the foothills that once hosted John and Jacqueline Kennedy for their honeymoon. Staying overnight is a budget-buster out of reach for most of us, but you can stroll the pretty grounds and enjoy comfort food in the ranch's rustic and cozy **Plow & Angel.** Warm your soul with a bowl of its famed tortilla soup. The mac and cheese, grilled burger, and martinis are also highly recommended.

Before planning your weekend, check the calendar for the **Santa Barbara Bowl** (1122 N. Milpas St., 805/962-7411, www.sbbowl.com) to see if there's a show you want to catch while in town. The outdoor venue is located in Santa Barbara's Milpas neighborhood. Whether you see a show or not, do as I and all my friends do before heading back to L.A. and join the queue for tacos at the neighborhood's **La Súper-Rica** (622 N. Milpas St., 805/963-4940); look for its groovy zigzag roof. I love the fish tacos, but you can't go wrong with anything on the menu. Then take a seat on the outdoor patio, where you'll be in the company of many others from near and far.

49 Take an art road trip in the Coachella Valley

Get Out of Town • Entertainment and Events • Art and Culture

Why Go: The free Desert X outdoor art exhibition thinks outside the museum box and affords the public a massive, multisensory playground.

Where: This event takes place in the Coachella Valley; past Desert X hubs have been located in Palm Springs, about 110 miles east of L.A. via I-10, as well as in Palm Desert and Indio just southeast.

Timing: Desert X takes place biannually in odd years around late winter/spring, with works displayed for several months (and a few remaining year-round). Palm Springs is about a two-hour drive from L.A.

When you're feeling the need to escape the confines of our crowded city streets and enclosed art spaces, the biennial **Desert X** (http://desertx.org, free) in the Coachella Valley welcomes you. The event is akin to an exciting scavenger art hunt, with 10-16 site-specific installations spread across the desert. As art does, the pieces will conjure a range of emotions—possibly amplified by the open space, as you travel miles and clock steps between each. You might stand in awe at the sheer scale of one piece and find yourself ambivalent at another after hiking a quarter mile over dry terrain with the wind whipping your hair and blowing sand across your face.

Since 2017, Desert X has featured the work of contemporary international artists and collectives, led by visionary artistic director Neville Wakefield, who is invested in curating art experiences outside of traditional museum settings. Climate change, immigration, land ownership, and social justice are among the themes that Desert X projects have touched upon—with the desert and its natural, unbounded landscape shaping each, both in its creation and audience experience. Some works are placed in easily accessible downtown Palm Springs, like Felipe Baeza's *Finding Home in My Own Flesh* (between the Hyatt Palm Springs and West Elm), a mural celebrating immigrants and queer people of color who are integral to the community; created for the 2021 edition of Desert X, it's now a permanent piece. Others

Desert X installation view of Cara Romero, *Jackrabbit, Cottontail & Spirits of the Desert*, 2019. Photography by Lance Gerber. Courtesy the artist and Desert X.

Desert X installation view of Felipe Baeza, *Finding Home in My Own Flesh*, 2021. Photography by Lance Gerber. Courtesy the artist and Desert X.

are situated in remoter corners of the Coachella Valley that visitors must venture by car to see. In 2019, Iván Argote's *A Point of View* featured five staircases with viewing platforms, arranged in a sundial formation near the Salton Sea, allowing visitors to see the landscape from different perspectives. That same year, Cara Romero's *Jackrabbit, Cottontail & Spirits of the Desert* displayed a photo series on billboards along the much-trafficked Gene Autry Trail, acknowledging the many Indigenous peoples of the area. And in 2021, Nicholas Galanin's *Never Forget,* situated off Highway 111 with Mount San Jacinto as its backdrop, mimicked the design of the Hollywood Sign, spelling out "Indian Land," to call out the desert's, and continent's, original caretakers.

Visitors can set their own self-guided itinerary using the Desert X app. An online map is also on the website, and printed maps are available at designated Desert X hubs during the event. Installations are generally viewable sunrise to sunset, and distances between them vary. Guided bus tours and customized tours are offered (see the Desert X website for more information and pricing on that year's offerings). You can also chat with trained docents,

Modernism Week in Palm Springs

When Desert X takes its yearly break, there's still art, design, and architecture to enjoy every February, when the 11-day **Modernism Week** (http://modernismweek.com) attracts thousands of midcentury lovers to Palm Springs for more than 350 events, including home and garden tours, film screenings, informative talks, and the must-visit **Palm Springs Modernism Show & Sale** (http://palmspringsmodernism.com), where you can shop highly curated 20th-century furniture and home decor from national and international exhibitors and dealers. Events (prices range) sell out fast, so plan ahead. With its popularity growing each year, the organizers have added a mini Fall Preview in October that lasts four days and is filled with more than 50 events.

who are on-site at most of the exhibits on Saturdays, to learn more about the work and the artists. If you're looking for accommodations, there are lots of local rentals available, and Desert X organizers also identify a range of traditional motel and hotel options (with promo discount codes) on the website. Wear comfortable walking shoes and bring water, since some sites involve walking across semi-long stretches of desert terrain. And since you'll be traveling by car to various locations, try to pack yours with others to enjoy the scenes with!

50 Captain your own boat on Lake San Marcos

Get Out of Town • Get Outside

Why Go: Nothing makes you feel farther from L.A. than piloting a pontoon among black swans.

Where: San Marcos, 100 miles south of L.A. via I-5 and Highway 78

Timing: It takes about two hours to drive from L.A. to Lake San Marcos. Venture here any time of year for a day or weekend. Book boats online 2-5 days in advance if you're planning a trip over a holiday.

For a peaceful getaway from the city, you don't need to drive hundreds of miles north to Lake Tahoe. In the San Diego suburb of San Marcos, you'll find a far easier to access, under-the-radar respite: the wonderfully serene Lake San Marcos. Situated on the northern tip of the lake, the 250-acre **Lakehouse Hotel & Resort** (1025 La Bonita Dr., 760/744-0120, marina bookings 760/621-0006, www.lakehousehotelandresort.com) serves as a base of operations. The now-hip boutique hotel, which underwent a makeover in 2014, has earned many fans, bringing an upscale, happening vibe to an area that was mostly known for its retirement community.

The lake's small, picture-perfect marina is managed by the resort and offers hotel guests as well as the public various ways to enjoy the water. While you can rent a stand-up paddleboard, kayak, water trike, or pedal boat, or even take a gondola cruise around the lake, it's the boat rentals that got my two sisters and our families excited. None of us had ever considered taking a large boat out on our own, anywhere—that's what other people do (you know, the ones who already own boats and have special boating licenses). But here, the bar of entry is low: All you need to rent a boat is a valid driver's license, to be 18 years of age or older, and to pay the boat rental fee ($100 per hour for a pontoon that seats up to seven, $120 per hour for a pontoon that seats up to 10). No prior experience is necessary, and a simple driving tutorial from one of the marina staff prepares you to get out on the water. I recommend bringing

1: food from Amalfi Marina Bar **2:** relaxing aboard a pontoon **3:** first-time boater enjoying the lake **4:** marina staff posing with Grandpa Bill, the senior black swan

drinks and snacks along on the ride, which you can pick up to go from one of the resort's four dining options.

As you pull away from the dock, expect to be joined by black and white swans; the black swans are especially friendly. Maybe you'll encounter the senior black swan, Grandpa Bill, also known by the locals as "King of Lake San Marcos," preening on the dock or hanging with the marina crew, who estimate he has been around for more than a decade. From the marina, head south toward the other end of the lake. You'll soon leave behind the hotel and lakefront houses, trading them in for vistas of green on both sides of the fairly narrow, 1.8-mile-long waterway. Park your boat near the lake's end for an extended period of time and you'll feel like you're on your own private body of water. Being on the open water, toasting the scene as the sun set, beers in hand (except for the pilot, of course) felt like a complete escape from our everyday big-city lives.

After the boat ride, consider dining dockside at the **Amalfi Marina Bar** (1035 La Bonita Dr., 760/653-3230, www.amalficucinaitaliana.com), where you'll find a lively crowd enjoy-

▲ dining dockside at the Amalfi Marina Bar

Lakehouse Hotel & Resort

ing the views. Our family enjoyed the Neapolitan-style pizzas, fish tacos, chocolate mousse cannoli, and Chantilly cake with berries.

Stay into the evening for other special attractions on the lakefront such as free movie nights, a nighttime fountain light show, and live music, or stay overnight at the resort. All reservations include some great complimentary items when you check in (subject to change) that might include an hour of stand-up paddleboarding or kayaking or a s'mores kit to use at the communal fire pits. If you come in a big group or are celebrating a special occasion and want to splurge, I highly recommend getting one of the spacious one- or two-bedroom cottages with lake view and private porch with fire pit.

51 Ride the *Pacific Surfliner* to Solana Beach

Get Out of Town • Get Outside • Shopping • For All Ages

Why Go: Enjoy front-row seats to SoCal scenes on the way to an idyllic beach town with a thriving design district.

Where: 102 miles south of L.A. • Amtrak *Pacific Surfliner* from Union Station to Solana Beach Station

Timing: The Amtrak ride takes about 2.5 hours, with nine trains running daily. Catch a morning train so you can spend the day. For a weekend jaunt, purchase tickets a few days in advance.

Amtrak's *Pacific Surfliner* (800/872-7245, www.pacificsurfliner.com) offers one of the most scenic rides in Southern California, covering 351 miles from San Luis Obispo to San Diego. On a train trip south from Los Angeles, riders get prime views of the lovely grit of our urban and industrial landscape—railyards, warehouses, overpasses, and graffiti-covered buildings—orderly suburban sprawl, chill beachside communities, and stretches of gorgeous undeveloped coastline.

A fun and easy way to experience the route is by taking a trip to San Diego County's **Solana Beach** (www.cityofsolanabeach.org), a charming coastal city; from the Amtrak station, you can walk right to the beach and a lively shopping district. Catching the *Pacific Surfliner* from L.A.'s historic **Union Station** (800 N. Alameda St., www.unionstationla.com, $62 round-trip coach ticket), open since 1939, is part of the adventure, as you join the rush of travelers walking (sometimes running) to their assigned boarding ramps. Once onboard, get a window seat facing west—ask the conductor which side to sit on—for the best coastal views.

Disembark at the **Solana Beach Station** (105 N. Cedros Ave.), a steel- and glass-heavy Quonset hut-inspired structure designed by local architect Rob Wellington Quigley. Upon arrival, you'll have a choice as to how to prioritize for the day: Head west for the beach or east for Solana's main shopping drag.

a magical sunset at Fletcher Cove Beach Park

Solana Beach Station

Amtrak's *Pacific Surfliner* traveling along the coastline

▲ Fletcher Cove Beach Park

A major attraction in Solana Beach is, aptly, its beaches. My pick is the **Fletcher Cove Beach Park** (111 S. Sierra Dr.), also known as **Pillbox,** just a five-minute walk from the station. Here, nestled between the bordering cliffs, you'll enjoy breathtaking ocean views, with a wide expanse of the Pacific before you. People come here to swim or boogie board or just sunbathe and lounge. The park also has a grassy area and playground. During summer, the city hosts outdoor **Concerts at the Cove** (Thurs., free) on a stage in the park. If you get hungry, just two blocks away is the unassuming **Sindi's Snack Shack** (132 S. Acacia Ave., 858/794-7071, www.sindissnackshack.com), which has a small patio area and a menu with items like Spam *musubi* (sticky rice with seaweed), banh mi sandwiches, and Korean street toast.

For shopping, head to the **Cedros Design District** (Cedros Ave. between Lomas Santa Fe Dr. and Marsolan Ave., 858/755-0444, http://cedrosavenue.com). It has more than 85 retailers, many of them independently owned, serving a mostly upscale clientele—furniture stores, art galleries, and specialty boutiques with inventory by local and international artisans—but it's also enjoyable to just meander and browse. Enjoy a snack, espresso, or organic meal at locally owned **Lofty Coffee Solana Beach** (132 S. Cedros Ave., 760/230-6747, www.loftycoffee.com). Then visit the outdoor garden at **Exclusive Collections** (212 S. Cedros Ave. #104, 619/650-3041, www.ecgallery.com), which is full of mesmerizing kinetic copper and steel wind sculptures by Lyman Whitaker. Check out the marquee at **Belly Up Tavern** (143 S. Cedros Ave., 858/451-8140, http://bellyup.com), dating to 1974. It collaborates with the city on Concerts at the Cove and here hosts many visiting indie rock bands; check to see if there's a show worth spending the night for. Just down the boulevard is my favorite store in all of San Diego County: the collective-run **SoLo** (309 S. Cedros Ave., 858/794-9016, www.solocedros.com), housed in a bright, wonderfully conceived warehouse space. Below its exposed wood beams, eight themed areas reflect the distinct tastes of its merchants, though they all flow together thanks to the thoughtful staging and custom tables made by local architect Jennifer Luce that help unify them. Founder Carole Carden, lover of all things midcentury modern, handpicked each merchant to focus on a specific category, including antiques and oddities, industrial furnishings, and coastal-inspired wares. Everywhere you turn, there's an item that demands attention: a pink neon Solana Beach sign, an exquisite layered-wood map, a vintage cake stand. Most of the shops in the Cedros Design District close at 5pm (or "whenever they feel like it," said one proprietor, who also noted that locals here "work to live" versus the other way around).

No matter where you started your day, be sure to circle back around to Fletcher Cove Beach Park for **sunset.**

For a meal before you head out, **Pillbox Tavern & Grill** (117 W. Plaza St., 858/436-7016, http://pillboxtavern.com) is near Fletcher Cove. The family-friendly restaurant has an outdoor patio where you can enjoy a tasty pulled pork sandwich and wings with a wide variety of sauces.

Amtrak's final departure from Solana back to L.A. is 9:40pm. Or, if you want to extend your trip, check in to the **Winner's Circle Resort** (550 Via de la Valle, 858/755-6666, www.winnerscircleresort.com), 1.5 miles south of Solana Beach Station.

52 Spend the night on Catalina Island

Get Out of Town • Get Outside • For All Ages

Why Go: An island getaway is just a ferry ride away from the city!

Where: Avalon, Santa Catalina Island • 310/510-1520 • www.lovecatalina.com

Timing: Plan for an overnight stay. Book ferry tickets and accommodations at least a week in advance for weekends and holidays. Two ferries depart daily from San Pedro to Avalon, and the ride takes 1.25 hours.

On a clear day, Angelenos can see the 76-square-mile **Santa Catalina Island**—more often simply called Catalina—from several vantages in the city. It's one of the spots residents point to as a metric for good weather or an incredible view: "You can see all the way to Catalina from here!" People can thank chewing gum magnate William Wrigley Jr., who purchased the island in 1919, for helping develop Catalina into a tourist destination, while ensuring, along with his descendants, that the majority of the island—almost 90 percent—would remain untouched. Adding further to the island's allure, bison, first introduced to the island in 1924 for a film shoot, roam free here.

 Catalina Express (310/519-7971, www.catalinaexpress.com) has daily high-speed ferries departing from the **Catalina Sea and Air Terminal** (Berth 95, Swinford St. and Harbor Blvd., parking $20 per day, round-trip ferry $76) in San Pedro, 25 miles south of Downtown L.A. On the way to Catalina, you may luck out and see dolphins!

 Avalon (www.cityofavalon.com) is the larger of the island's two seaport villages, the other being Two Harbors. Exuding small-town charm, it's located on the eastern end of Catalina, just 22 miles from "overtown," as locals like to call the mainland. From the dock at Avalon Bay, it's a five-minute walk along Pebbly Beach Road to the city's public beaches: **South Beach** and, on the other side of the pier, **Middle Beach,** dotted with people swimming, sunbathing, or reading a book.

 Running alongside the waterfront is the quaint village's main drag, **Crescent Avenue,**

biking on the island

Green Pleasure Pier

Avalon

entrance to the art deco Catalina Casino

Catalina Pottery & Tile Company

on the Discover Avalon tour

lined with souvenir and specialty shops and eateries. Definitely stop by **Catalina Island Conservancy's Trailhead** (708 Crescent Ave., 310/510-2595, http://catalinaconservancy. org), which provides complimentary maps as well as a handful of educational multimedia displays about the island. As a child, I particularly enjoyed watching saltwater taffy being made in the window at **Lloyd's of Avalon** (315 Crescent Ave., 310/510-7266, http://catalinacandy.com), open since 1954, where you can shop an assortment of candy. As an adult, **Catalina Pottery & Tile Company** (523 Crescent Ave., 310/510-1937, http://catalinapotteryandtile.com) appeals, with locally made wares featuring beautifully designed tiles and pottery, both new and vintage, as well as jewelry and artisan food items. You'll notice that tile decorates the island, from storefronts to beach benches.

A nice way to get acquainted with the area is the 50-minute, open-air **Discover Avalon** (800/626-1496, www.visitcatalinaisland.com) shuttle tour that winds through the village and up into the foothills. Check to see when Bear is working, as he offers an especially entertaining mix of history and humor! You'll learn interesting history about the island, which was first inhabited by Native Americans some 8,000 years ago and called Pimu, and enjoy beautiful views as you ride along the sometimes narrow, steep roads.

The number of cars on the island is limited, so you won't find Ubers or Lyfts here, though you can rent a golf cart, the locals' preferred method of travel. But Avalon is small, just over 2.8 square miles, and easy to get around by foot or bike; you can rent beach cruisers, e-bikes, mountain bikes, and tandem bikes from the friendly folks at **Brown's Bikes** (107 Pebbly Beach Rd., 310/510-0986, http://catalinabiking.com).

Whether you're walking or cycling, do some exploring along the coastline. From Brown's Bikes, it's just under a mile north along the waterfront to the happening **Descanso Beach Club** (1 St. Catherine Way, 877/778-8322, www.visitcatalinaisland.com), just past the island's most prominent architectural landmark, the 1929 art deco **Catalina Casino** (1 Casino Way, 310/510-0179). The casino has its own private beach and a restaurant and bar packed with people socializing on sunny days on spacious decks overlooking the water. Here you can enjoy such signature Catalina drinks as the Descanso Destroyer (orange and pineapple juices, rum, amaretto) and Buffalo Milk (crème de cacao, banana liqueur, Patrón XO Café, milk). Don't be surprised to encounter deer grazing near the club.

Or head south along the coastline from Brown's Bikes for a peaceful ride or walk and photo ops at spots like **Lover's Cove Scenic Vista** and **Abalone Point.** Just over a mile south is **Silver Canyon Pottery** (22 Pebbly Beach Rd., 310/499-8799, www.catalinatile-experience.com), where you can learn about the colorful tiles that decorate the island and create your own if you like.

Whichever part of the coast you hit, head back into town and then inland via Sumner Avenue and Avalon Canyon Road; it's an uphill 15-minute bike ride with a downhill reward or a 30-minute walk to the **Wrigley Memorial and Botanic Garden** (1400 Avalon Canyon Rd., 310/510-2987). Completed in 1934, the monument recognizes the many contributions of Wrigley Jr., and his wife, Ada. Catch expansive views of Avalon Bay as you wander the nearly 38-acre garden, which includes many rare plants. On your way back down, stop at **The Sandtrap Restaurant and Bar** (501 Avalon Canyon Rd., 310/510-2505) to catch its happy hour (2pm-7pm daily), featuring drink specials and $2 tacos.

Back in the village, if you're ready for dinner, order anything on the menu at seafood

▲ The Lobster Trap (mural by artist Jason Greene)

stop **The Lobster Trap** (128 Catalina Ave., 310/510-8585, www.catalinalobstertrap.com). You can find shots, fun raffles, and a party atmosphere at **The Locker Room Sports Bar** (126 Sumner Ave., 310/510-0258), housed in the locker room once used by the Chicago Cubs when they trained on the island.

Many of the properties on the island are owned by Catalina Island Company; my pick for accommodations on a recent trip was **Pavilion Hotel** (513 Crescent Ave., 310/510-1788, www.visitcatalinaisland.com), which has many perks, including a complimentary wine and cheese reception and discounts on company tours and activities, such as kayaking, zip lining, an aerial adventure course, and boating—enough to fill days if you have extra time.

For breakfast the next day, head to longtime eatery **The Pancake Cottage** (618 Crescent Ave., 310/510-0726, http://thepancakecottagecatalina.com). Or go for some avocado toast and a street corn salad at **Café Metropole** (113 Metropole Ave., 310/510-9095, http://cafemetropole.com).

For people-watching entertainment or to while away some time before your departure, head to **Green Pleasure Pier** (Crescent St. and Catalina Ave.), where seagulls keep watch as throngs of people from ferries arrive or depart throughout the day and then disappear. During such intervals, the streets are so empty that you'll feel like the island is yours.

Connect with . . .

🔵 Picnic and park-hop in seaside San Pedro

INDEX

ACKNOWLEDGMENTS

I wrote this book during one of the most trying times in our history. Thousands who were part of the fabric of this city lost their lives. This book is dedicated to them and the frontliners, community groups, volunteers, agencies, leaders, and educators without whom this city would not still beat with the energy, hope, and drive to persist in such ever-changing circumstances.

The land I inhabit and the sites featured in this book are on the ancestral and unceded territory of the Gabrielino/Tongva peoples—the traditional caretakers of Tovaangar (Los Angeles Basin and southern Channel Islands)—and their neighbors. I pay my respects to its members, their families, and elders—past, present, and emerging—who have cared for these lands for thousands of years, still call it home, and remain stewards and advocates, educating generations about the landscape and its gifts to ensure the welfare of its peoples and all who live here.

Thank you to the communities, neighborhoods, and dreamers of L.A.—you are the heart and soul of the city.

My utmost gratitude goes to everyone at Moon, especially acquisitions editor Nikki Ioakimedes for embracing my L.A. experiences and helping them shine in my proposal; book editor Kristi Mitsuda for being supportive throughout and thoughtfully making every word matter; and production coordinator Rue Flaherty, map editor Albert Angulo, and cartographer John Culp for making this book as visually rich and layered as the city.

Thank you, family and friends, for joining me on endless adventures—the good, the challenging, and the thrilling. Your shared love for (or aversion to) the city has strengthened my deep attachment to it! This is my hometown because my *lolo* and *lola* immigrated here in search of a different life, and my parents followed them with their own dreams. I treasure the decades we spent at the family home in East Hollywood, where three generations of Apeleses gathered, partied, and feasted.

To the numerous locals and visitors I met—especially the friendly strangers on the street—who guided and inspired me with their personal stories and recommendations as I navigated the city, your contributions are priceless. Also, a big shout-out to my multilingual friends for helping us communicate when I didn't have the words.

This book wouldn't be what it is without the amazing editors and collaborators I've had over the years, and the photographers, artists, entrepreneurs, artisans, performers, and activists who allowed me to share their work.

During the course of writing this book, some whose legacies are represented on these pages passed away—from a Tongva elder who did art workshops with young adults in Downtown to a Haitian-born sommelier who cofounded a wine store in West Adams to a newly appointed leader in Historic Filipinotown whose organization serves hundreds of families each year. You will not be forgotten.

For the wildlife and public spaces (especially our parks and libraries), may you remain protected and free.

To Los Angeles, for all the drama and heartbreak you bring that have yet to outweigh the joys—you are my forever home.

And, to you, dear readers, for embarking on these journeys. As my cousin Jin would say, "Let's make memories . . ."

PHOTO CREDITS

MURAL CREDITS:

page 4 (bottom), 83 (top left): *Gintong Kasaysayan, Gintong Pamana* ("A Glorious History, A Golden Legacy," 1995) by Eliseo Art Silva. FilAm Arts, Kayamanan Ng Lahi, and Malaya Filipino American Dance Arts performers in the foreground.

page 53 (top): detail of *Great Wall of Los Angeles* mural: *Legend of Califa, Indigenous Perspective, Junipero Sera,* and *Founders of Los Angeles* designed by Judith F. Baca; page 53 (bottom) *Chinese Build the Railroad* and *Chinese Massacre 1871,* designed by Gary Takamoto; page 54 (bottom) *Big Mama Thornton, Forebears of Civil Rights,* and *Gay Rights* designed by Judith F. Baca with the support of Matt Weurker, Jan Cook, and additional SPARC design team members.

page 183 (bottom right): *Una Trenza* (Self Help Graphics & Art mural) by Vyal Reyes, Leo Limon, Wayne Perry, The Esparza Family (Ofelia Esparza, Rosanna Esparza-Ahrens, Jacqueline "Jaxiejax" Sanders-Esparza, Elena Esparza), Los de Abajo (Poli Marichal, Don Newton, Kay Brown, Nguyen Li, Victor Rosas, Marianne Sadowski), Yolanda Gonzalez, John Carlos de Luna, William Acedo, Asylm, Margaret Alarcon, Fabian Debora, Ricardo Estrada, Raul Gonzalez, Sand, and Raul Baltazar.